CSS Fonts

Eric A. Meyer

Beijing · Cambridge · Farnham · Köln · Sebastopol · Tokyo

CSS Fonts

by Eric A. Meyer

Published by O'Reilly Media, Inc., 1005 Gravenstein Highway North, Sebastopol, CA 95472.

O'Reilly books may be purchased for educational, business, or sales promotional use. Online editions are also available for most titles (*http://my.safaribooksonline.com*). For more information, contact our corporate/institutional sales department: 800-998-9938 or *corporate@oreilly.com*.

Editors: Simon St. Laurent and Meghan Blanchette	**Cover Designer:** Randy Comer
Production Editor: Kristen Borg	**Interior Designer:** David Futato
Proofreader: O'Reilly Production Services	**Illustrator:** Rebecca Demarest

July 2013:   First Edition

Revision History for the First Edition:

2013-07-16:   First release

See *http://oreilly.com/catalog/errata.csp?isbn=9781449371494* for release details.

ISBN: 978-1-449-37149-4

[LSI]

Table of Contents

Preface

Conventions Used in This Book

The following typographical conventions are used in this book:

Italic
> Indicates new terms, URLs, email addresses, filenames, and file extensions.

`Constant width`
> Used for program listings, as well as within paragraphs to refer to program elements such as variable or function names, databases, data types, environment variables, statements, and keywords.

`Constant width bold`
> Shows commands or other text that should be typed literally by the user.

`Constant width italic`
> Shows text that should be replaced with user-supplied values or by values determined by context.

 This icon signifies a tip, suggestion, or general note.

 This icon indicates a warning or caution.

Safari® Books Online

 Safari Books Online (*www.safaribooksonline.com*) is an on-demand digital library that delivers expert content in both book and video form from the world's leading authors in technology and business.

Technology professionals, software developers, web designers, and business and creative professionals use Safari Books Online as their primary resource for research, problem solving, learning, and certification training.

Safari Books Online offers a range of product mixes and pricing programs for organizations, government agencies, and individuals. Subscribers have access to thousands of books, training videos, and prepublication manuscripts in one fully searchable database from publishers like O'Reilly Media, Prentice Hall Professional, Addison-Wesley Professional, Microsoft Press, Sams, Que, Peachpit Press, Focal Press, Cisco Press, John Wiley & Sons, Syngress, Morgan Kaufmann, IBM Redbooks, Packt, Adobe Press, FT Press, Apress, Manning, New Riders, McGraw-Hill, Jones & Bartlett, Course Technology, and dozens more. For more information about Safari Books Online, please visit us online.

How to Contact Us

Please address comments and questions concerning this book to the publisher:

> O'Reilly Media, Inc.
> 1005 Gravenstein Highway North
> Sebastopol, CA 95472
> 800-998-9938 (in the United States or Canada)
> 707-829-0515 (international or local)
> 707-829-0104 (fax)

We have a web page for this book, where we list errata, examples, and any additional information. You can access this page at *http://oreil.ly/css-fonts_1e*.

To comment or ask technical questions about this book, send email to *bookquestions@oreilly.com*.

For more information about our books, courses, conferences, and news, see our website at *http://www.oreilly.com*.

Find us on Facebook: *http://facebook.com/oreilly*

Follow us on Twitter: *http://twitter.com/oreillymedia*

Watch us on YouTube: *http://www.youtube.com/oreillymedia*

Fonts

As the authors of CSS clearly recognized from the outset, font selection is a popular, indeed crucial, feature of web design. In fact, the beginning of the "Font Properties" section of the CSS1 specification begins with the sentence, "Setting font properties will be among the most common uses of style sheets." The intervening years have done nothing to disprove this assertion.

CSS2 added the ability to specify custom fonts for download with @font-face, but it wasn't until about 2009 that this capability really began to be widely and consistently supported. Now, websites can call on any font they have the right to use, aided by online services such as Fontdeck and Typekit. Generally speaking, if you can get access to a font, you can use it in your design.

It's important to remember, however, that this does not grant absolute control over fonts. If the font you're using fails to download or is in a file format the user's browser doesn't understand, then the text will be displayed with a fallback font. That's a good thing, since it means the user still gets your content, but it's worth bearing in mind that you cannot absolutely depend on the presence of a given font, and should never design as if you can.

Font Families

What we think of as a "font" is usually composed of many variations to describe bold text, italic text, and so on. For example, you're probably familiar with (or at least have heard of) the font Times. However, Times is actually a combination of many variants, including TimesRegular, TimesBold, TimesItalic, TimesBoldItalic, and so on. Each of these variants of Times is an actual *font face*, and Times, as we usually think of it, is a combination of all these variant faces. In other words, Times is actually a *font family*, not just a single font, even though most of us think about fonts as being single entities.

In order to cover all the bases, CSS defines five generic font families:

Serif fonts

> These fonts are proportional and have serifs. A font is proportional if all characters in the font have different widths due to their various sizes. For example, a lowercase *i* and a lowercase *m* are different widths. (This book's paragraph font is proportional, for example.) Serifs are the decorations on the ends of strokes within each character, such as little lines at the top and bottom of a lowercase *l*, or at the bottom of each leg of an uppercase *A*. Examples of serif fonts are Times, Georgia, and New Century Schoolbook.

Sans-serif fonts

> These fonts are proportional and do not have serifs. Examples of sans-serif fonts are Helvetica, Geneva, Verdana, Arial, and Univers.

Monospace fonts

> Monospace fonts are not proportional. These generally are used for displaying programmatic code or tabular data. In these fonts, each character uses up the same amount of horizontal space as all the others; thus, a lowercase *i* takes up the same horizontal space as a lowercase *m*, even though their actual letterforms may have different widths. These fonts may or may not have serifs. If a font has uniform character widths, it is classified as monospace, regardless of the presence of serifs. Examples of monospace fonts are Courier, Courier New, Consolas, and Andale Mono.

Cursive fonts

> These fonts attempt to emulate human handwriting or lettering. Usually, they are composed largely of flowing curves and have stroke decorations that exceed those found in serif fonts. For example, an uppercase *A* might have a small curl at the bottom of its left leg or be composed entirely of swashes and curls. Examples of cursive fonts are Zapf Chancery, Author, and Comic Sans.

Fantasy fonts

> Such fonts are not really defined by any single characteristic other than our inability to easily classify them in one of the other families (these are sometimes called "decorative" or "display" fonts). A few such fonts are Western, Woodblock, and Klingon.

In theory, every font family will fall into one of these generic families. In practice, this may not be the case, but the exceptions (if any) are likely to be few and far between, and browsers are likely to drop any fonts they cannot classify as serif, sans-serif, monospace, or cursive into the "fantasy" bucket.

Using Generic Font Families

You can employ any font family available by using the property `font-family`.

---

font-family

Values:
   [*<family-name>* | *<generic-family>*]# | inherit

Initial value:
   User agent-specific

Applies to:
   All elements

Inherited:
   Yes

Computed value:
   As specified

If you want a document to use a sans-serif font, but you do not particularly care which one, then the appropriate declaration would be:

```
body {font-family: sans-serif;}
```

This will cause the user agent to pick a sans-serif font family (such as Helvetica) and apply it to the body element. Thanks to inheritance, the same font family choice will be applied to all the elements that descend from the body—unless a more specific selector overrides it, of course.

Using nothing more than these generic families, an author can create a fairly sophisticated style sheet. The following rule set is illustrated in Figure 1:

```
body {font-family: serif;}
h1, h2, h3, h4 {font-family: sans-serif;}
code, pre, tt, kbd {font-family: monospace;}
p.signature {font-family: cursive;}
```

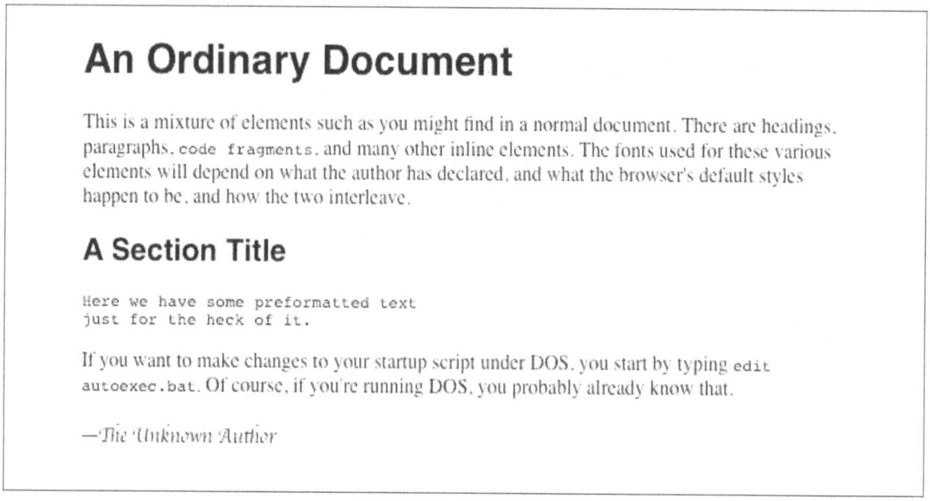

An Ordinary Document

This is a mixture of elements such as you might find in a normal document. There are headings, paragraphs, `code fragments`, and many other inline elements. The fonts used for these various elements will depend on what the author has declared, and what the browser's default styles happen to be, and how the two interleave.

A Section Title

```
Here we have some preformatted text
just for the heck of it.
```

If you want to make changes to your startup script under DOS, you start by typing `edit autoexec.bat`. Of course, if you're running DOS, you probably already know that.

—The Unknown Author

Figure 1. Various font families

Thus, most of the document will use a serif font such as Times, including all paragraphs except those that have a `class` of `signature`, which will instead be rendered in a cursive font such as Author. Heading levels 1 through 4 will use a sans-serif font like Helvetica, while the elements `code`, `pre`, `tt`, and `kbd` will use a monospace font like Courier.

Specifying a Font Family

An author may, on the other hand, have more specific preferences for which font to use in the display of a document or element. In a similar vein, a user may want to create a user style sheet that defines the exact fonts to be used in the display of all documents. In either case, `font-family` is still the property to use.

Assume for the moment that all `h1`s should use Georgia as their font. The simplest rule for this would be the following:

```
h1 {font-family: Georgia;}
```

This will cause the user agent displaying the document to use Georgia for all `h1`s, as shown in Figure 2.

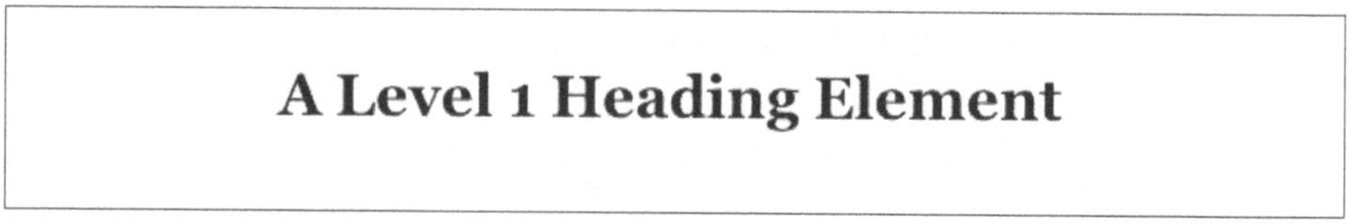

Figure 2. An h1 element using Georgia

Of course, this rule assumes that the user agent has Georgia available for use. If it doesn't, the user agent will be unable to use the rule at all. It won't ignore the rule, but if it can't find a font called "Georgia," it can't do anything but display h1 elements using the user agent's default font (whatever that is).

All is not lost, however. By combining specific font names with generic font families, you can create documents that come out, if not exact, at least close to your intentions. To continue the previous example, the following markup tells a user agent to use Georgia if it's available, and to use another serif font if it's not.

```
h1 {font-family: Georgia, serif;}
```

If a reader doesn't have Georgia installed but does have Times, the user agent might use Times for h1 elements. Even though Times isn't an exact match to Georgia, it's probably close enough.

For this reason, I strongly encourage you to always provide a generic family as part of any font-family rule. By doing so, you provide a fallback mechanism that lets user agents pick an alternative when they can't provide an exact font match. Here are a few more examples:

```
h1 {font-family: Arial, sans-serif;}
h2 {font-family: Charcoal, sans-serif;}
p {font-family: 'Times New Roman', serif;}
address {font-family: Chicago, sans-serif;}
```

If you're familiar with fonts, you might have a number of similar fonts in mind for displaying a given element. Let's say that you want all paragraphs in a document to be displayed using Times, but you would also accept Times New Roman, Georgia, New Century Schoolbook, and New York (all of which are serif fonts) as alternate choices. First, decide the order of preference for these fonts, and then string them together with commas:

```
p {font-family: Times, 'Times New Roman', 'New Century Schoolbook', Georgia,
   'New York', serif;}
```

Based on this list, a user agent will look for the fonts in the order they're listed. If none of the listed fonts are available, then it will simply pick an available serif font.

Using quotation marks

You may have noticed the presence of single quotes in the previous example, which we haven't seen before. Quotation marks are advisable in a font-family declaration only if a font name has one or more spaces in it, such as "New York," or if the font name includes symbols such as # or $. Thus, a font called Karrank% should probably be quoted:

```
h2 {font-family: Wedgie, 'Karrank%', Klingon, fantasy;}
```

If you leave off the quotation marks, there is a chance that user agents will ignore that particular font name altogether, although they'll still process the rest of the rule.

Note that the quoting of a font name containing a symbol is not actually required any more. Instead, it's recommended, which is as close to describing "best practices" as the CSS specification ever really gets. Similarly, it is recommended that you quote a font name containing spaces, though again, this is generally unnecessary in modern user agents. As it turns out, the only required quotation is for font names that match accepted font-family keywords. Thus, if you call for a font whose actual name is "cursive," you'll definitely need to quote it in order to distinguish it from the value keyword cursive:

```
h2 {font-family: Author, "cursive", cursive;}
```

Obviously, font names that use a single word (that doesn't conflict with any of the keywords for font-family) need not be quoted, and generic family names (serif, monospace, etc.) should never be quoted when they refer to the actual generic families. If you quote a generic name, then the user agent will assume that you are asking for a specific font with that name (for example, "serif"), not a generic family.

As for which quotation marks to use, both single and double quotes are acceptable. Remember that if you place a font-family rule in a style attribute, which you generally shouldn't, you'll need to use whichever quotes you didn't use for the attribute itself. Therefore, if you use double quotes to enclose the font-family rule, then you'll have to use single quotes within the rule, as in the following markup:

```
p {font-family: sans-serif;}  /* sets paragraphs to sans-serif by default */

<!-- the next example is correct (uses single-quotes) -->
<p style="font-family: 'New Century Schoolbook', Times, serif;">...</p>

<!-- the next example is NOT correct (uses double-quotes) -->
<p style="font-family: "New Century Schoolbook", Times, serif;">...</p>
```

If you use double quotes in such a circumstance, they interfere with the attribute syntax, as you can see in Figure 3.

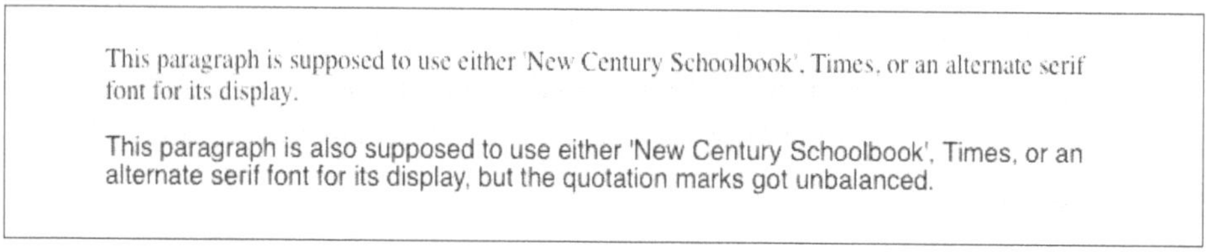

This paragraph is supposed to use either 'New Century Schoolbook', Times, or an alternate serif font for its display.

This paragraph is also supposed to use either 'New Century Schoolbook', Times, or an alternate serif font for its display, but the quotation marks got unbalanced.

Figure 3. The perils of incorrect quotation marks

Using @font-face

A feature that originally debuted in CSS2 but wasn't implemented until late in the first decade of the 2000s, @font-face lets you use custom fonts in your designs. While there's no guarantee that every last user will see the font you want, this feature is very widely supported and (as of early 2013) gaining a lot of currency in web design.

Suppose you want to use a very specific font in your style sheets, one that is not widely installed. Through the magic of @font-face, you can define a specific family name to correspond to a font file on your server. The user agent will download that file and use it to render the text in your page, the same as if it were installed on the user's machine. For example:

```
@font-face {
    font-family: "SwitzeraADF";
    src: url("SwitzeraADF-Regular.otf");
}
```

This allows the author to have conforming user agents load the defined .otf file and use that font to render text when called upon via font-family: SwitzeraADF.

 The examples in this section refer to SwitzeraADF, a font face collection available from the Arkandis Digital Foundry (*http://arkandis.tuxfamily.org/openfonts.html*).

The intent of @font-face is to allow "lazy loading" of font faces. This means that only those faces needed to render a document will actually be loaded, with the rest being left alone. In fact, a browser that downloads all declared font faces without considering whether they're actually needed is considered to be buggy.

Required Descriptors

All the parameters that define the font you're referencing are contained within the @font-face { } construct. These are called *descriptors*, and very much like properties, they take the format descriptor: value;. In fact, most of the descriptor names refer directly to property names, as will be explained in just a moment.

There are two required descriptors: font-family and src.

font-family

Value:
    <family-name>

Initial value:
    Not defined

src

Values:
    `[ [ ` *<uri>* ` [format(` *<string>* `#)]? ] | ` *<font-face-name>* ` ]#`

Initial value:
    Not defined

The point of `src` is pretty straightforward: it lets you define one or more sources for the font face you're defining, using a comma-separated list if there are in fact multiple sources. You can point to a font face at any URI, but there is a restriction: font faces can only be loaded from the same origin as the style sheet. Thus, you can't point your `src` at someone else's site and download their font; you'll need to host a local copy on your own server, or use a font-hosting service that provides both the style sheet(s) and the font file(s).

 There is an exception to the same-origin restriction, which is that servers can permit cross-site loading using the HTTP header `Access-Control-Allow-Origin`.

You may well be wondering how it is that we're defining `font-family` here when it was already defined in a previous section. The difference is that this `font-family` is the font-family *descriptor*, and the previously-defined `font-family` was the font-family *property*. If that seems confusing, stick with me a moment and all should become clear.

In effect, `@font-face` lets you create low-level definitions that underpin the font-related properties like `font-family`. When you define a font family name via the descriptor `font-family: "SwitzeraADF";`, you're setting up an entry in the user agent's table of font families for "SwitzeraADF." It thus joins all the usual suspects like Helvetica, Georgia, Courier, and so forth, as a font you can just refer to in your `font-family` property values.

```
@font-face {
    font-family: "SwitzeraADF";    /* descriptor */
    src: url("SwitzeraADF-Regular.otf");
}
h1 {font-family: SwitzeraADF, Helvetica, sans-serif;}  /* property */
```

Note how the font-family descriptor value and the entry in the font-family property match. If they didn't match, then the h1 rule would ignore the first font family name listed in the font-family value and move on to the next. As long as the font has cleanly downloaded and is in a format the user agent can handle, then it will be used in the manner you direct, as illustrated in Figure 4.

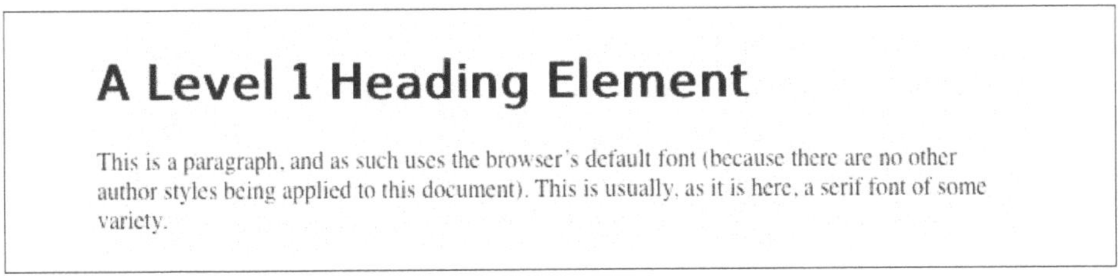

A Level 1 Heading Element

This is a paragraph, and as such uses the browser's default font (because there are no other author styles being applied to this document). This is usually, as it is here, a serif font of some variety.

Figure 4. Using a downloaded font

In a similar manner, the comma-separated src descriptor value provides fallbacks. That way, if (for whatever reason) the user agent is unable to download the first source, it can fall back to the second source and try to load the file there.

```
@font-face {
    font-family: "SwitzeraADF";
    src: url("SwitzeraADF-Regular.otf"),
         url("/fonts/SwitzeraADF-Regular.otf");
}
```

Remember that the same-origin policy generally applies in this case, so pointing to a copy of the font some other server will usually fail, unless of course said server is set up to permit cross-origin access.

If you want to be sure the user agent understands what kind of font you're telling it to use, that can be done with the optional format().

```
@font-face {
    font-family: "SwitzeraADF";
    src: url("SwitzeraADF-Regular.otf") format("opentype");
}
```

The advantage of supplying a format() description is that user agents can skip downloading files in formats that they don't support, thus reducing bandwidth use and loading speed. It also lets you explicitly declare a format for a file that might not have a common filename extension and thus be unfamiliar to the user agent.

```
@font-face {
    font-family: "SwitzeraADF";
    src: url("SwitzeraADF-Regular.otf") format("opentype"),
         url("SwitzeraADF-Regular.true") format("truetype");
}
```

The Flash

If you're a designer or developer of a certain vintage, you may remember the days of FOUC: the Flash of Unstyled Content. This happened in earlier browsers that would load the HTML and display it to the screen before the CSS was finished loading, or at least before the layout of the page via CSS was finished. Thus, what would appear was a split-second of "plain ol' text" (using the browser's default styles) before it was replaced with the CSS-decorated layout.

As of early 2013, there is a cousin to this problem, which is the Flash of Un-Fonted Text, or FOUFT. This happens when a browser has loaded the page and the CSS and displays the laid-out page before it's done loading custom fonts. This causes text to appear in the default font, or a fallback font, before being replaced by text using the custom-loaded font.

Since the replacement of text with the custom-loaded font face can change its layout size, authors should take care in selecting fallback fonts. If there is a significant height difference between the font used to initially display the text and the custom font eventually loaded and used, significant page reflows are likely to occur. There's no automated way to enforce this, though font-size-adjust (covered later) can help. You simply have to look at your intended font and find other faces that have a similar height.

The core reason for the "flash" behavior is pretty much the same now as it was then: the browser is ready to show something before it has all the resources on hand, so it goes ahead and does so, replacing it with the prettier version once it can. The FOUC was eventually solved, and it's likely that some day we'll look back at the FOUFT the same way we do at the FOUC now. Until then, we'll have to take comfort in the fact that the FOUFT isn't usually as jarring as was the FOUC.

Table 1 lists all of the allowed format values (as of early 2013).

Table 1. Recognized font format values

Value	Format
embedded-opentype	EOT (Embedded OpenType)
opentype	OTF (OpenType)
svg	SVG (Scalable Vector Graphics)
truetype	TTF (TrueType)
woff	WOFF (Web Open Font Format)

In addition to the combination of `url()` and `format()`, you can also supply a font family name (or several names) in case the font is already locally available on the user's machine, using the aptly-named `local()`.

```
@font-face {
    font-family: "SwitzeraADF";
    src: local("Switzera-Regular"),
        local("SwitzeraADF-Regular "),
        url("SwitzeraADF-Regular.otf") format("opentype"),
        url("SwitzeraADF-Regular.true") format("truetype");
}
```

In this example, the user agent looks to see if it already has a font family named "Switzera-Regular" or "SwitzeraADF-Regular" available. If so, it will use the name `SwitzeraADF` to refer to that locally installed font. If not, it will use the `url()` value to try downloading the remote font.

Note that this capability allows an author to create custom names for locally installed fonts. For example, you could set up a shorter name for Helvetica (or, failing that, Helvetica Neue) like so:

```
@font-face {
    font-family: "H";
    src: local("Helvetica"),
        local("Helvetica Neue");
}

h1, h2, h3 {font-family: H, sans-serif;}
```

As long as the user has Helvetica installed on their machine, then those rules will cause the first three heading levels to be rendered using Helvetica. It seems a little gimmicky, but it could have a real impact on reducing style sheet file size in certain situations.

On Being Bulletproof

The tricky part with `@font-face` is that different browsers of different eras supported different font formats. (To the insider, Table 1 reads as a capsule history of downloadable font support.) In order to cover the widest possible landscape, you should turn to what is known as the "Bulletproof `@font-face` Syntax." Initially developed by Paul Irish and refined by the chaps at FontSpring, it looks like this:

```
@font-face {
    font-family: "SwitzeraADF";
    src: url("SwitzeraADF-Regular.eot");
    src: url("SwitzeraADF-Regular.eot?#iefix") format("embedded-opentype"),
        url("SwitzeraADF-Regular.woff") format("woff"),
        url("SwitzeraADF-Regular.ttf") format("truetype"),
        url("SwitzeraADF-Regular.svg#switzera_adf_regular") format("svg");
}
```

Let's break it down piece by piece. The first bit, assigning the `font-family` name, is straightforward enough. After that, we see:

```
src: url("SwitzeraADF-Regular.eot");
    src: url("SwitzeraADF-Regular.eot?#iefix") format("embedded-opentype"),
```

This supplies an EOT (Embedded OpenType) to browsers that understand only EOTs—IE6 through IE9. The first line is for IE9 when it's in "Compatibility Mode," and the second line hands the same file to IE6-IE8. The `?#iefix` bit in that line exploits a parsing bug in those browsers to step around another parsing bug that causes them to 404 any `@font-face` with multiple formats listed. IE9 fixed its bugs without expanding its font formats, so the first line is what lets it join the party.

```
url("SwitzeraADF-Regular.woff") format("woff"),
```

This line supplies a Web Open Font Format file to browsers that understand it, which includes most modern browsers. At this point, in fact, you'll have covered the vast majority of your desktop users.

```
url("SwitzeraADF-Regular.ttf") format("truetype"),
```

This line hands over the file format understood by most iOS and Android devices, thus covering most of your handheld users.

```
url("SwitzeraADF-Regular.svg#switzera_adf_regular") format("svg");
```

Here, at the end, we supply the only font format understood by old iOS devices. This covers almost all of your remaining handheld users.

Obviously, this gets a bit unwieldy if you're specifying more than a couple of faces, and typing it in even once is kind of a pain in the wrists. Fortunately, there are services available that will accept your font faces and generate all the `@font-face` rules you need, convert those faces to all the formats required, and hand it all back to you as a single package. One of the best is Font Squirrel's "@Font-Face Kit Generator" (*http://fonts quirrel.com/fontface/generator*). Just make sure you're legally able to convert and use the font faces you're running through the generator (see the next sidebar, "Custom Font Considerations", for more information).

Other Font Descriptors

In addition to the required `font-family` and `src` descriptors, there are a number of optional descriptors that can be used to associate font faces with specific font property values. Just as with `font-family`, these descriptors (summarized in Table 2) correspond directly to CSS properties (explained in detail later in this chapter) and affect how user agents respond to the values supplied for those properties.

Custom Font Considerations

There are two things you need to keep in mind when using customized fonts. The first is that you have the rights to use the font in a web page, and the second is whether it's a good idea to do so.

Much like stock photography, font families come with licenses that govern their use, and not every font license permits its use on the web. You can completely avoid this question by only using FOSS (Free and Open-Source Software) fonts only, or by using a commercial service like Fontdeck or Typekit that will deal with the licensing and format conversion issues so you don't have to. Otherwise, you need to make sure that you have the right to use a font face in the way you want to use it, just the same as you would make sure you had the proper license for any images you bought.

In addition, the more font faces you call upon, the more resources the web server has to hand over and the higher the overall page weight will become. Most faces are not overly large—usually 50K to 100K—but they add up quickly if you decide to get fancy with your type, and truly complicated faces can be larger. Of course, the same problems exist for images. As always, you will have to balance appearance against performance, leaning one way or the other depending on the circumstances. Furthermore, just as there are image optimization tools available, there are also font optimization tools. Typically these are "subsetting" tools, which construct fonts using only the symbols actually needed for display. If you're using a service like Typekit or Fonts.com, they probably have subsetting tools available, or do it dynamically when the font is requested.

Table 2. Font descriptors

Descriptor	Default value	Description
font-style	normal	Distinguishes between normal, italic, and oblique faces
font-weight	normal	Distinguishes between various weights (e.g., bold)
font-stretch	normal	Distinguishes between varying degrees of character widths (e.g., condensed and expanded)
font-variant	normal	Distinguishes between a staggeringly wide range of potential variant faces (e.g., small-caps); in most ways, a more "CSS-like" version of font-feature-settings
font-feature-settings	normal	Permits direct access to low-level OpenType features (e.g., enabling ligatures)
unicode-range	U+0-10FFFF	Defines the range of characters for which a given face may be used

Because these font descriptors are optional, they may not be listed in a `@font-face` rule, but CSS does not allow descriptors to go without default values any more than it does for properties. If an optional descriptor is omitted, then it is set to the default value. Thus, if `font-weight` is not listed, the default value of `normal` is assumed.

Restricting Character Range

There is one font descriptor, `unicode-range`, which (unlike the others in Table 2) has no corresponding CSS property. This descriptor allows authors to define the range of characters to which a custom font can be applied. This can be useful when using a symbol font, or to ensure that a font face is only applied to characters that are in a specific language.

---

unicode-range

Values:
    <urange>#

Initial value:
    U+0-10FFFF

By default, the value of this property covers the entirety of Unicode, meaning that if a font can supply the glyph for a character, it will. Most of the time, this is exactly what you want. For all the other times, you'll want to use a specific font face for a specific kind of content. To pick two examples from the CSS Fonts Module Level 3:

```
unicode-range: U+590-5FF;   /* Hebrew characters */
unicode-range: U+4E00-9FFF, U+FF00-FF9F, U+30??;   /* Japanese kanji, hiragana,
katakana */
```

In the first case, a single range is specified, spanning Unicode character code point 590 through code point 5FF. This covers the characters used in Hebrew. Thus, an author might specify a Hebrew font and restrict it to only be used for Hebrew characters, even if the face contains glyphs for other code points:

```
@font-face {
    font-family: "CMM-Ahuvah";
    src: url("cmm-ahuvah.otf" format("opentype");
    unicode-range: U+590-5FF;
}
```

In the second case, a series of ranges are specified in a comma-separated list to cover all the Japanese characters. The interesting feature there is the U+30?? value, which is a special format permitted in `unicode-range` values. The question marks are wildcards meaning "any possible digit," making U+30?? equivalent to U+3000-30FF. The question mark is the only "special" character pattern permitted in the value.

Ranges must always ascend. Any descending range (e.g., U+400-300) is treated as a parsing error and ignored. Besides ranges, you can also declare a single code point, which looks like U+221E. This is most often useful in conjunction with other code points and ranges, like so:

```
unicode-range: U+4E00-9FFF, U+FF00-FF9F, U+30??, U+A5;
    /* Japanese kanji, hiragana, and katakana, plus yen/yuan currency symbol*/
```

Of course, you could use a single code point to declare that a specific face only be used to render one, and only one, character. Whether or not that's a good idea is left to you, your design, the size of the font file, and your users' connection speeds.

Because @font-face is designed for "lazy loading" optimization, it's possible to use unicode-range to download only the font faces a page actually needs. Suppose that you have a website that uses a mixture of English, Russian, and basic mathematical operators, but you don't know which will appear on any given page. There could be all English, a mixture of Russian and math, and so on. Furthermore, suppose you have special font faces for all three types of content. You can make sure a user agent only downloads the faces it actually needs with a properly-constructed series of @font-face rules.

```
@font-face {
    font-family: "MyFont";
    src: url("myfont-general.otf") format("opentype");
}
@font-face {
    font-family: "MyFont";
    src: url("myfont-cyrillic.otf") format("opentype");
    unicode-range: U+04??, U+0500-052F, U+2DE0-2DFF, U+A640-A69F, U+1D2B-1D78;
}
@font-face {
    font-family: "MyFont";
    src: url("myfont-math.otf") format("opentype");
    unicode-range: U+22??;          /* equivalent to U+2200-22FF */
}
```

Because the first rule doesn't specify a Unicode range, it is always downloaded—unless, of course, a page happens to contain no characters at all (and maybe even then). The second rule causes myfont-cyrillic.otf to be downloaded only if the page contains characters in its declared Unicode range; the third rule does the same for basic mathematical operators.

 As of mid-2013, the only user agent line to support unicode-range was the Webkit family.

Combining Descriptors

Something that might not be immediately obvious is that you can supply multiple descriptors in order to assign specific faces for specific property combinations. For example, you can assign one face to bold text, another to italic text, and a third to text that is both bold and italic.

This is actually implicit in the fact that any undeclared descriptor is assigned its default value. Let's consider a basic set of three face assignments:

```
@font-face {
    font-family: "SwitzeraADF";
    font-weight: normal;
    font-style: normal;
    font-stretch: normal;
    src: url("SwitzeraADF-Regular.otf") format("opentype");
}
@font-face {
    font-family: "SwitzeraADF";
    font-weight: bold;
    font-style: normal;
    font-stretch: normal;
    src: url("SwitzeraADF-Bold.otf") format("opentype");
}
@font-face {
    font-family: "SwitzeraADF";
    font-weight: normal;
    font-style: italic;
    font-stretch: normal;
    src: url("SwitzeraADF-Italic.otf") format("opentype");
}
```

Here, we've made the implicit explicit: any time a descriptor isn't being altered, its default value is listed. This is exactly the same as a set of three rules in which we remove every descriptor that shows a value of normal:

```
@font-face {
    font-family: "SwitzeraADF";
    src: url("SwitzeraADF-Regular.otf") format("opentype");
}
@font-face {
    font-family: "SwitzeraADF";
    font-weight: bold;
    src: url("SwitzeraADF-Bold.otf") format("opentype");
}
@font-face {
    font-family: "SwitzeraADF";
    font-style: italic;
    src: url("SwitzeraADF-Italic.otf") format("opentype");
}
```

In all three rules, there is no font-stretching beyond the normal amount, and the values of `font-weight` and `font-style` vary by which face is being assigned. So what if we want to assign a specific face to unstretched text that's both bold and italic?

```
@font-face {
    font-family: "SwitzeraADF";
    font-weight: bold;
    font-style: italic;
    font-stretch: normal;
    src: url("SwitzeraADF-BoldItalic.otf") format("opentype");
}
```

And then what about bold, italic, condensed text?

```
@font-face {
    font-family: "SwitzeraADF";
    font-weight: bold;
    font-style: italic;
    font-stretch: condensed;
    src: url("SwitzeraADF-BoldCondItalic.otf") format("opentype");
}
```

How about normal-weight, italic, condensed text?

```
@font-face {
    font-family: "SwitzeraADF";
    font-weight: normal;
    font-style: italic;
    font-stretch: condensed;
    src: url("SwitzeraADF-CondItalic.otf") format("opentype");
}
```

We could keep this up for quite a while, but let's stop there. If we take all those rules and strip out anything with a `normal` value, we end up with this result, illustrated in Figure 5:

```
@font-face {
    font-family: "SwitzeraADF";
    src: url("SwitzeraADF-Regular.otf") format("opentype");
}
@font-face {
    font-family: "SwitzeraADF";
    font-weight: bold;
    src: url("SwitzeraADF-Bold.otf") format("opentype");
}
@font-face {
    font-family: "SwitzeraADF";
    font-style: italic;
    src: url("SwitzeraADF-Italic.otf") format("opentype");
}
@font-face {
    font-family: "SwitzeraADF";
    font-weight: bold;
    font-style: italic;
    src: url("SwitzeraADF-BoldItalic.otf") format("opentype");
}
```

```
}
@font-face {
    font-family: "SwitzeraADF";
    font-weight: bold;
    font-stretch: condensed;
    src: url("SwitzeraADF-BoldCond.otf") format("opentype");
}
@font-face {
    font-family: "SwitzeraADF";
    font-style: italic;
    font-stretch: condensed;
    src: url("SwitzeraADF-CondItalic.otf") format("opentype");
}
@font-face {
    font-family: "SwitzeraADF";
    font-weight: bold;
    font-style: italic;
    font-stretch: condensed;
    src: url("SwitzeraADF-BoldCondItalic.otf") format("opentype");
}
```

This element contains serif text, unstretched **bold** and *italic* text in SwitzeraADF, and unstretched ***bold and italic*** text in SwitzeraADF.

This element contains serif text, condensed **bold** and *italic* text in SwitzeraADF, and condensed ***bold and italic*** text in SwitzeraADF.

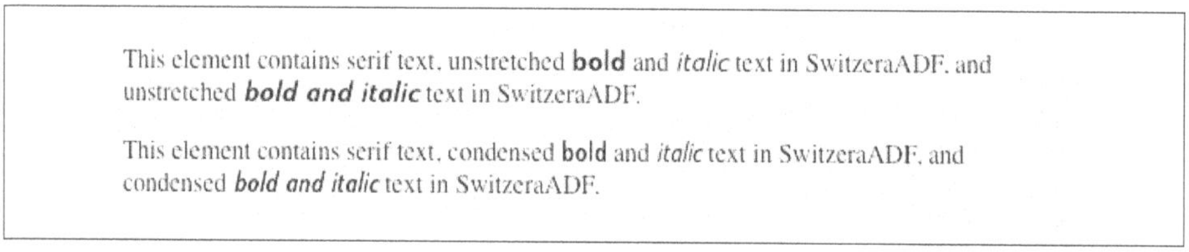

Figure 5. Employing a variety of faces

As you can see, there are a lot of possible combinations just for those three descriptors —consider that there are eleven possible values for font-weight, and ten for font-stretch—but you'll likely never have to run through them all. In fact, most font families don't have as many faces as SwitzeraADF offers (24 at last count) so there wouldn't be much point in writing out all the possibilities. Nevertheless, the options are there, and in some cases you may find that you need to assign, say, a specific face for bold condensed text so that the user agent doesn't try to compute them for you.

Font Weights

Now that we've covered @font-face and its descriptors, let's get back to properties. We're all used to normal and bold text, at the very least, which are sort of the two most basic font weights available. CSS gives you a lot more control over font weights with the property font-weight.

font-weight

Values:
    normal | bold | bolder | lighter | 100 | 200 | 300 | 400 | 500 | 600 | 700 | 800 | 900
    | inherit

Initial value:
    normal

Applies to:
    All elements

Inherited:
    Yes

Computed value:
    One of the numeric values (100, etc.), or one of the numeric values plus one of the
    relative values (bolder or lighter)

Note:
    Has a corresponding @font-face descriptor (see below)

Generally speaking, the heavier a font weight becomes, the darker and "more bold" a font appears. There are a great many ways to label a heavy font face. For example, the font family known as SwitzeraADF has a number of variants, such as SwitzeraADF Bold, SwitzeraADF Extra Bold, SwitzeraADF Light, and SwitzeraADF Regular. All of these use the same basic font shapes, but each has a different weight.

So let's say that you want to use SwitzeraADF for a document, but you'd like to make use of all those different heaviness levels. You could refer to them directly through the font-family property, but you really shouldn't have to do that. Besides, it's no fun having to write a style sheet like this:

```
h1 {font-family: 'SwitzeraADF Extra Bold, sans-serif;}
h2 {font-family: 'SwitzeraADF Bold, sans-serif;}
h3 {font-family: 'SwitzeraADF Bold', sans-serif;}
h4, p {font-family: SwitzeraADF Regular, sans-serif;}
small {font-family: 'SwitzeraADF Light', sans-serif;}
```

That's pretty tedious. It would make far more sense to specify a single font family for the whole document and then assign different weights to various elements. You can do this via @font-face and use the various values for the property font-weight. This is a fairly obvious font-weight declaration:

```
b {font-weight: bold;}
```

This declaration says, simply, that the b element should be displayed using a bold font face; or, to put it another way, a font face that is heavier than the normal font face. This is what we're used to, of course, since b does cause text to be bold.

What's really happening behind the scenes is that a heavier face of the font is used for displaying a b element. Thus, if you have a paragraph displayed using Times, and part of it is bold, then there are really two faces of the same font in use: Times and TimesBold. The regular text is displayed using Times, and the bold text is displayed using TimesBold.

How Weights Work

To understand how a user agent determines the heaviness, or weight, of a given font variant (not to mention how weight is inherited), it's easiest to start by talking about the keywords 100 through 900. These number keywords were defined to map to a relatively common feature of font design in which a font is given nine levels of weight. If a font family has faces for all nine weight levels available, then the numbers are mapped directly to the predefined levels, with 100 as the lightest variant of the font and 900 as the heaviest.

In fact, there is no intrinsic weight in these numbers. The CSS specification says only that each number corresponds to a weight at least as heavy as the number that precedes it. Thus, 100, 200, 300, and 400 might all map to the same relatively lightweight variant; 500 and 600 could correspond to the same heavier font variant; and 700, 800, and 900 could all produce the same very heavy font variant. As long as no keyword corresponds to a variant that is lighter than the variant assigned to the previous keyword, everything will be all right.

As it happens, these numbers are defined to be equivalent to certain common variant names, not to mention other values for font-weight. 400 is defined to be equivalent to normal, and 700 corresponds to bold. The other numbers do not match up with any other values for font-weight, but they can correspond to common variant names. If there is a font variant labeled something such as "Normal," "Regular," "Roman," or "Book," then it is assigned to the number 400 and any variant with the label "Medium" is assigned to 500. However, if a variant labeled "Medium" is the only variant available, it is assigned to 400 instead of 500.

A user agent has to do even more work if there are fewer than nine weights in a given font family. In this case, it must fill in the gaps in a predetermined way:

- If the value 500 is unassigned, it is given the same font weight as that assigned to 400.
- If 300 is unassigned, it is given the next variant lighter than 400. If no lighter variant is available, 300 is assigned the same variant as 400. In this case, it will usually be "Normal" or "Medium." This method is also used for 200 and 100.

- If 600 is unassigned, it is given the next variant darker than that assigned for 500. If no darker variant is available, 600 is assigned the same variant as 500. This method is also used for 700, 800, and 900.

To illustrate this weighting scheme more clearly, let's look at three examples of font weight assignment. In the first example, assume that the font family Karrank% is an OpenType font, so it has nine weights already defined. In this case, the numbers are assigned to each level, and the keywords normal and bold are assigned to the numbers 400 and 700, respectively. This is the most straightforward example, and therefore the one that almost never occurs in the real world. (It is quite rare for a font family to have nine weight levels, and those that do are usually very expensive.)

In our second example, consider the font family SwitzeraADF, which was discussed near the beginning of this section. Hypothetically, its variants might be assigned numeric values for font-weight, as shown in Table 3.

Table 3. Hypothetical weight assignments for a specific font family

Font face	Assigned keyword	Assigned number(s)
SwitzeraADF Light		100, 200, 300
SwitzeraADF Regular	normal	400
SwitzeraADF Medium		500
SwitzeraADF Bold	bold	600, 700
SwitzeraADF Extra Bold		800, 900

The first three number values are assigned to the lightest weight. The "Regular" face gets the keyword normal, as expected, and the number weight 400. Since there is a "Medium" font, it's assigned to the number 500. There is nothing to assign to 600, so it's mapped to the "Bold" font face, which is also the variant to which 700 and bold are assigned. Finally, 800 and 900 are assigned to the "Black" and "UltraBlack" variants, respectively. Note that this last assignment would happen only if those faces had the top two weight levels already assigned. Otherwise, the user agent might ignore them and assign 800 and 900 to the "Bold" face instead, or it might assign them both to one or the other of the "Black" variants.

For our third and final example, let's consider a stripped-down version of Times. In Table 4, there are only two weight variants: "TimesRegular" and "TimesBold."

Table 4. Hypothetical weight assignments for "Times"

Font face	Assigned keyword	Assigned numbers
TimesRegular	normal	100, 200, 300, 400, 500
TimesBold	bold	600, 700, 800, 900

The assignment of the keywords normal and bold is straightforward enough, of course. As for the numbers, 100 through 300 are assigned to the "Regular" face because there isn't a lighter face available. 400 is assigned to "Regular" as expected, but what about 500? It is assigned to the "Regular" (or normal) face because there isn't a "Medium" face available; thus, it is assigned the same font face as 400. As for the rest, 700 goes with bold as always, while 800 and 900, lacking a heavier face, are assigned to the next-lighter face, which is the "Bold" font face. Finally, 600 is assigned to the next-heavier face, which is, of course, the "Bold" face.

font-weight is inherited, so if you set a paragraph to be bold:

```
p.one {font-weight: bold;}
```

...then all of its children will inherit that boldness, as we see in Figure 6.

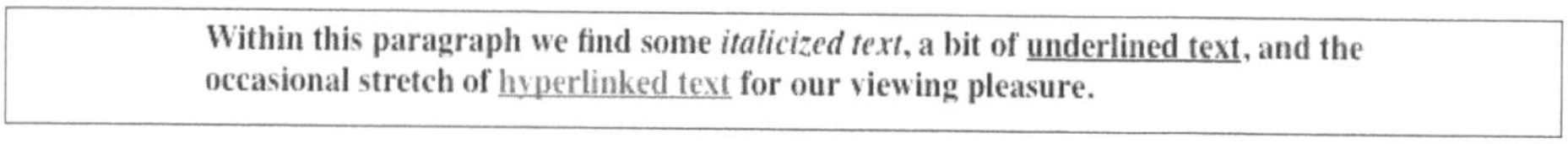

Within this paragraph we find some *italicized text*, a bit of underlined text, and the occasional stretch of hyperlinked text for our viewing pleasure.

Figure 6. Inherited font-weight

This isn't unusual, but the situation gets interesting when you use the last two values we have to discuss: bolder and lighter. In general terms, these keywords have the effect you'd anticipate: they make text more or less bold compared to its parent's font weight. First, let's consider bolder.

Getting Bolder

If you set an element to have a weight of bolder, then the user agent first must determine what font-weight value was inherited from the parent element. It then selects the lowest number which corresponds to a font weight darker than what was inherited. If none is available, then the user agent sets the element's font weight to the next numerical value, unless the value is already 900, in which case the weight remains at 900. Thus, you might encounter the following situations, illustrated in Figure 7:

```
p {font-weight: normal;}
p em {font-weight: bolder;}  /* results in bold text, evaluates to '700' */

h1 {font-weight: bold;}
h1 b {font-weight: bolder;}  /* if no bolder face exists, evaluates to '800' */

div {font-weight: 100;} /* assume 'Light' face exists; see explanation */
div strong {font-weight: bolder;} /* results in normal text, weight '400' */
```

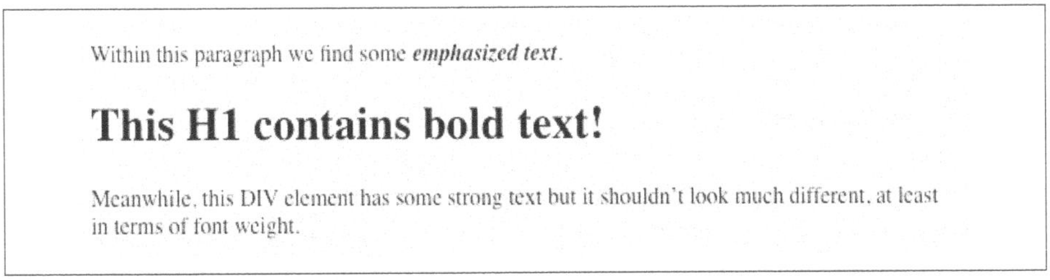

Within this paragraph we find some *emphasized text*.

This H1 contains bold text!

Meanwhile, this DIV element has some strong text but it shouldn't look much different, at least in terms of font weight.

Figure 7. Text trying to be bolder

In the first example, the user agent moves up the weight ladder from normal to bold; in numeric terms, it jumps from 400 to 700. In the second example, h1 text is already set to bold. If there is no bolder face available, then the user agent sets the weight of b text within an h1 to 800, since that is the next step up from 700 (the numeric equivalent of bold). Since 800 is assigned to the same font face as 700, there is no visible difference between normal h1 text and bold h1 text, but the weights are different nonetheless.

In the last example, paragraphs are set to be the lightest possible font weight, which we assume exists as a "Light" variant. Furthermore, the other faces in this font family are "Regular" and "Bold." Any em text within a paragraph will evaluate to normal since that is the next-heaviest face within the font family. However, what if the only faces in the font are "Regular" and "Bold"? In that case, the declarations would evaluate like this:

```
/*   assume only two faces for this example: 'Regular' and 'Bold'   */
p {font-weight: 100;}   /* looks the same as 'normal' text */
p span {font-weight: bolder;}   /* maps to '700' */
```

As you can see, the weight 100 is assigned to the normal font face, but the value of font-weight is still 100. Thus, any span text that is descended from a p element will inherit the value of 100 and then evaluate to the next-heaviest face, which is the "Bold" face with a numerical weight of 700.

Let's take this one step further and add two more rules, plus some markup, to illustrate how all of this works (see Figure 8 for the results):

```
/*   assume only two faces for this example: 'Regular' and 'Bold'   */
p {font-weight: 100;}   /* looks the same as 'normal' text */
p span {font-weight: 400;}   /* so does this */
strong {font-weight: bolder;}   /* even bolder than its parent */
strong b {font-weight: bolder;}   /*bolder still */

<p>
This paragraph contains elements of increasing weight: there is a
<span>span element that contains a <strong>strongly emphasized
element and a <b>bold element</b></strong></span>.
</p>
```

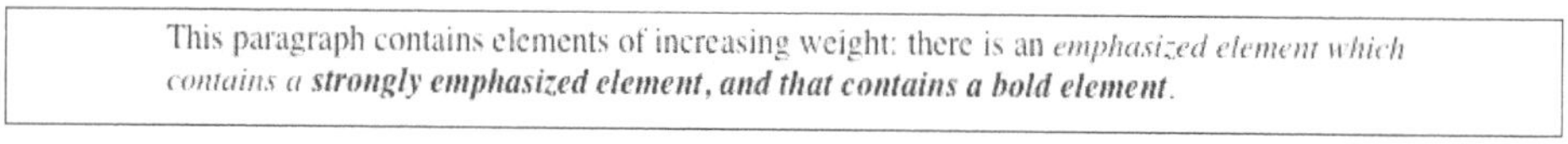

> This paragraph contains elements of increasing weight: there is an *emphasized element which contains a* **strongly emphasized element, and that contains a bold element**.

Figure 8. Moving up the weight scale

In the last two nested elements, the computed value of font-weight is increased because of the liberal use of the keyword bolder. If you were to replace the text in the paragraph with numbers representing the font-weight of each element, you would get the results shown here:

```
<p>
100 <span> 400 <strong> 700 <b> 800 </b> </strong> </span>.
</p>
```

The first two weight increases are large because they represent jumps from 100 to 400 and from 400 to bold (700). From 700, there is no heavier face, so the user agent simply moves the value of font-weight one notch up the numeric scale (800). Furthermore, if you were to insert a strong element into the b element, it would come out like this:

```
<p>
100 <span> 400 <strong> 700 <b> 800 <strong> 900
</strong> </b> </strong> </span>.
</p>
```

If there were yet another b element inserted into the innermost strong element, its weight would also be 900, since font-weight can never be higher than 900. Assuming that there are only two font faces available, then the text would appear to be either Regular or Bold, as you can see in Figure 9:

```
<p>
regular <span> regular <strong> bold <b> bold <strong> bold </strong> </b>
</strong> </span>.
</p>
```

> 100 *400* **700 800** .

Figure 9. Visual weight, with descriptors

Lightening Weights

As you might expect, lighter works in just the same way, except it causes the user agent to move down the weight scale instead of up. With a quick modification of the previous example, you can see this very clearly:

```
/*   assume only two faces for this example: 'Regular' and 'Bold'   */
p {font-weight: 900;}   /* as bold as possible, which will look 'bold' */
p span {font-weight: 700;}   /* this will also be bold */
strong {font-weight: lighter;}   /* lighter than its parent */
b {font-weight: lighter;}   /* lighter still */
```

```
<p>
900 <span> 700 <strong> 400 <b> 300 <strong> 200
</strong> </b> </strong> </span>.
</p>
<!-- ...or, to put it another way... -->
<p>
bold <span> bold <strong> regular <b> regular <strong> regular </strong></b>
</strong></span>.
</p>
```

Ignoring the fact that this would be entirely counterintuitive, what you see in Figure 10 is that the main paragraph text has a weight of 900. When the `strong` text is set to be `lighter`, it evaluates to the next-lighter face, which is the regular face, or 400 (the same as `normal`) on the numeric scale. The next step down is to 300, which is the same as `normal` since no lighter faces exist. From there, the user agent can reduce the weight only one numeric step at a time until it reaches 100 (which it doesn't do in the example). The second paragraph shows which text will be bold and which will be regular.

---

900 700 400 300 200 .

Figure 10. Making text lighter

The font-weight Descriptor

With the `font-weight` descriptor, authors can assign faces of varying weights to the weighting levels permitted by the `font-weight` property. For example, the following rules explicitly assign five faces to six different `font-weight` values:

```
@font-face {
    font-family: "SwitzeraADF";
    font-weight: normal;
    src: url("f/SwitzeraADF-Regular.otf") format("opentype");
}
@font-face {
    font-family: "SwitzeraADF";
    font-weight: bold;
    src: url("f/SwitzeraADF-Bold.otf") format("opentype");
}
@font-face {
    font-family: "SwitzeraADF";
    font-weight: 300;
    src: url("f/SwitzeraADF-Light.otf") format("opentype");
}
@font-face {
    font-family: "SwitzeraADF";
    font-weight: 500;
    src: url("f/SwitzeraADF-DemiBold.otf") format("opentype");
}
```

```
@font-face {
    font-family: "SwitzeraADF";
    font-weight: 700;
    src: url("f/SwitzeraADF-Bold.otf") format("opentype");
}
@font-face {
    font-family: "SwitzeraADF";
    font-weight: 900;
    src: url("f/SwitzeraADF-ExtraBold.otf") format("opentype");
}
```

With these faces assigned, the author now has a number of weighting levels available for his use, as illustrated in Figure 11:

```
h1, h2, h3, h4 {font: 225% SwitzeraADF, Helvetica, sans-serif;}
h1 {font-weight: 900;}
h2 {font-size: 180%; font-weight: 700;}
h3 {font-size: 150%; font-weight: 500;}
h4 {font-size: 125%; font-weight: 300;}
```

Figure 11. Using declared font-weight faces

In any given situation, the user agent picks which face to use depending on the exact value of a font-weight property, using the resolution algorithm detailed earlier in this section. Authors may use any value for the font-weight descriptor that is permitted for the font-weight property *except* the inherit keyword.

Font Size

The methods for determining font size are both very familiar and very different.

font-size

Values:
    xx-small|x-small|small|medium|large|x-large|xx-large|smaller|larger | <length> | <percentage> | inherit

Initial value:
    medium

Applies to:
    All elements

Inherited:
    Yes

Percentages:
    Calculated with respect to the parent element's font size

Computed value:
    An absolute length

In a fashion very similar to the font-weight keywords bolder and lighter, the property font-size has relative-size keywords called larger and smaller. Much like what we saw with relative font weights, these keywords cause the computed value of font-size to move up and down a scale of size values, which you'll need to understand before you can explore larger and smaller. First, though, we need to examine how fonts are sized in the first place.

In fact, the actual relation of the font-size property to what you see rendered is determined by the font's designer. This relationship is set as an *em square* (some call it an *em box*) within the font itself. This em square (and thus the font size) doesn't have to refer to any boundaries established by the characters in a font. Instead, it refers to the distance between baselines when the font is set without any extra leading (line-height in CSS). It is quite possible for fonts to have characters that are taller than the default distance between baselines. For that matter, a font might be defined such that all of its characters are smaller than its em square, as many fonts do. Some hypothetical examples are shown in Figure 12.

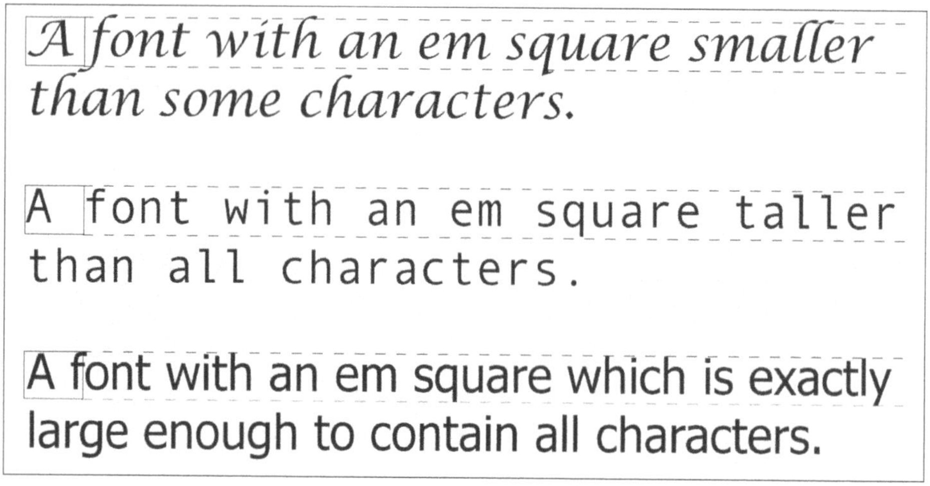

Figure 12. Font characters and em squares

Thus, the effect of `font-size` is to provide a size for the em box of a given font. This does not guarantee that any of the actual displayed characters will be this size.

Absolute Sizes

Having established all of that, we turn now to the absolute-size keywords. There are seven absolute-size values for `font-size`: xx-small, x-small, small, medium, large, x-large, and xx-large. These are not defined precisely, but are relative to each other, as Figure 13 demonstrates:

```
p.one {font-size: xx-small;}
p.two {font-size: x-small;}
p.three {font-size: small;}
p.four {font-size: medium;}
p.five {font-size: large;}
p.six {font-size: x-large;}
p.seven {font-size: xx-large;}
```

According to the CSS1 specification, the difference (or *scaling factor*) between one absolute size and the next is about 1.5 going up the ladder, or 0.66 going down. Thus, if medium is the same as 10px, then large should be the same as 15px. This was later determined to be too large a scaling factor. In CSS2 it was suggested that it be somewhere between 1.0 and 1.2, and in CSS3 drafts a complicated series is provided (for example, small is listed as 8/9ths the size of medium, while xx-small is 3/5ths). In all case, the scaling factors are guidelines, as user agents are free to alter them for any reason.

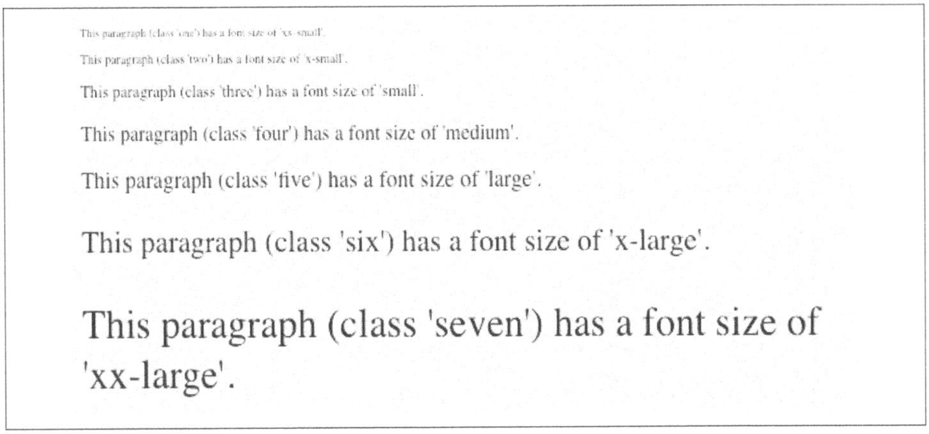

This paragraph (class 'one') has a font size of 'xx-small'.

This paragraph (class 'two') has a font size of 'x-small'.

This paragraph (class 'three') has a font size of 'small'.

This paragraph (class 'four') has a font size of 'medium'.

This paragraph (class 'five') has a font size of 'large'.

This paragraph (class 'six') has a font size of 'x-large'.

This paragraph (class 'seven') has a font size of 'xx-large'.

Figure 13. Absolute font sizes

Working from the assumption that `medium` equals `16px`, for different scaling factors, we get the absolute size equivalents shown in Table 5. (The values shown are rounded-off integers.)

Table 5. Scaling factors translated to pixels

Keyword	CSS1	CSS2	CSS3 (draft)
xx-small	5px	9px	10px
x-small	7px	11px	12px
small	11px	13px	14px
medium	16px	16px	16px
large	24px	19px	19px
x-large	36px	23px	24px
xx-large	54px	28px	32px

Relative Sizes

Comparatively speaking, the keywords `larger` and `smaller` are simple: they cause the size of an element to be shifted up or down the absolute-size scale, relative to their parent element, using the same scaling factor employed to calculate absolute sizes. In other words, if the browser used a scaling factor of 1.2 for absolute sizes, then it should use the same factor when applying relative-size keywords:

```
p {font-size: medium;}
strong, em {font-size: larger;}

<p>This paragraph element contains <strong>a strong-emphasis element
which itself contains <em>an emphasis element that also contains
<strong>a strong element.</strong></em></strong></p>
```

```
<p> medium <strong>large <em> x-large <strong>xx-large</strong> </em> </strong>
</p>
```

Unlike the relative values for weight, the relative-size values are not necessarily constrained to the limits of the absolute-size range. Thus, a font's size can be pushed beyond the sizes for xx-small and xx-large. For example:

```
h1 {font-size: xx-large;}
em {font-size: larger;}

<h1>A Heading with <em>Emphasis</em> added</h1>
<p>This paragraph has some <em>emphasis</em> as well.</p>
```

As you can see in Figure 14, the emphasized text in the h1 element is slightly larger than xx-large. The amount of scaling is left up to the user agent, with the scaling factor of 1.2 being preferred but not required. The em text in the paragraph, of course, is shifted one slot up the absolute-size scale (large).

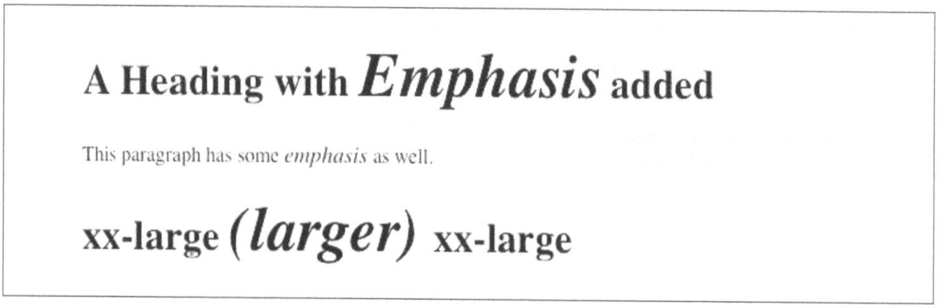

A Heading with *Emphasis* added

This paragraph has some *emphasis* as well.

xx-large *(larger)* xx-large

Figure 14. Relative font sizing at the edges of the absolute sizes

User agents are not required to increase or decrease font size beyond the limits of the absolute-size keywords.

Percentages and Sizes

In a way, percentage values are very similar to the relative-size keywords. A percentage value is always computed in terms of whatever size is inherited from an element's parent. Percentages, unlike the size keywords previously discussed, permit much finer control over the computed font size. Consider the following example, illustrated in Figure 15:

```
body {font-size: 15px;}
p {font-size: 12px;}
em {font-size: 120%;}
strong {font-size: 135%;}
small, .fnote {font-size: 70%;}
```

```
<body>
<p>This paragraph contains both <em>emphasis</em> and <strong>strong
emphasis</strong>, both of which are larger than their parent element.
The <small>small text</small>, on the other hand, is smaller by a quarter.</p>
<p class="fnote">This is a 'footnote' and is smaller than regular text.</p>

<p> 12px <em> 14.4px </em> 12px <strong> 16.2px </strong> 12px
<small> 9px </small> 12px </p>
<p class="fnote"> 10.5px </p>
</body>
```

Figure 15. Throwing percentages into the mix

In this example, the exact pixel size values are shown. These are the values calculated by the browser, regardless of the actual displayed size of the characters on-screen.

Incidentally, CSS defines the length value em to be equivalent to percentage values, in the sense that 1em is the same as 100% when sizing fonts. Thus, the following would yield identical results, assuming that both paragraphs have the same parent element:

```
p.one {font-size: 166%;}
p.two {font-size: 1.6em;}
```

When using em measurements, the same principles apply as with percentages, such as the inheritance of computed sizes and so forth.

Font Size and Inheritance

Figure 12 also demonstrates that, although font-size is inherited in CSS, it is the computed values that are inherited, not percentages. Thus, the value inherited by the strong element is 12px, and this value is modified by the declared value 135% to arrive at 16.2px. For the "footnote" paragraph, the percentage is calculated in relation to the font-size value that's inherited from the body element, which is 15px. Multiplying that value by 75% yields 11.25px.

As with the relative-size keywords, percentages are effectively cumulative. Thus, the following markup is displayed as shown in Figure 16:

```
p {font-size: 12px;}
em {font-size: 120%;}
strong {font-size: 135%;}
```

```
<p>This paragraph contains both<em>emphasis and <strong>strong
emphasis</strong></em>, both of which are larger than the paragraph text. </p>

<p> 12px <em>14.4px <strong> 19.44px </strong></em> 12px  </p>
```

Figure 16. The issues of inheritance

The size value for the strong element shown in Figure 16 is computed as follows:

12 px × 120% = 14.4px
14.4px × 135% = 19.44px (possibly rounded to 19px for display; see below)

The problem of runaway scaling can go the other direction, too. Consider for a moment a document that is nothing but a series of unordered lists, many of them nested inside other lists. Some of these lists are four nested levels deep. Imagine the effect of the following rule on such a document:

```
ul {font-size: 80%;}
```

Assuming a four-level deep nesting, the most deeply nested unordered list would have a computed font-size value 40.96 percent the size of the parent of the top-level list. Every nested list would have a font size 80 percent as big as its parent list, causing each level to become harder and harder to read.

Rounding for Display

In most modern browsers, while fractional font-size values are maintained internally, they are not always used by rendering engines. For example, study the letterforms in Figure 17.

In all cases, the "O" characters increase by 0.1 pixels in size as you go from left to right. Thus, the leftmost "O" has a font-size of 10px, the one at the midpoint has a size of 10.5px, and the one on the right is 11px.

As Figure 17 reveals, different browser/OS combinations yield different results. For example, Opera, Safari, and Chrome for OS X show an abrupt jump from 10 pixels to 11 pixels at the 10.5px position. Internet Explorer and Firefox for Windows (both 7 and 8) do the same. Firefox for OS X, on the other hand, looks like it has a smooth line of same-size text. In fact, the characters are all being drawn subtly differently, thanks to their subtly different font-size values. It's hard to see without squinting (or a ruler), but the fact that it's hard to tell that there is an increase in size from one end of the line to the other is evidence enough.

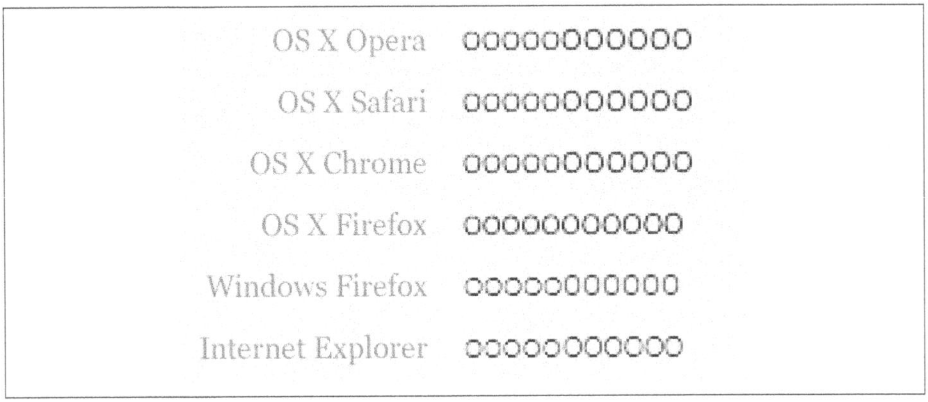

OS X Opera	OOOOOOOOOOO
OS X Safari	OOOOOOOOOOO
OS X Chrome	OOOOOOOOOOO
OS X Firefox	OOOOOOOOOOO
Windows Firefox	OOOOOOOOOOO
Internet Explorer	OOOOOOOOOOO

Figure 17. Fractional font sizes

Nevertheless, every browser will yield up the same subpixel font-size values if you use an inspector or query the value directly via DOM scripting. The third "O" from the right will show a computed value of 10.8px, regardless of the size of the character displayed on-screen.

Keywords and Monospace Text

There's an interesting wrinkle to font size keywords and inheritance that becomes apparent when you look at what some browsers do with monospace text (e.g., Courier). Consider the following, illustrated in Figure 18:

```
p {font-size: medium;}   /* the default value */
span {font-family: monospace; font-size: 1em;}

<p>This is a 'p' with a <span>'span'</span> inside.</p>
```

This is a 'p' with a `span` inside.

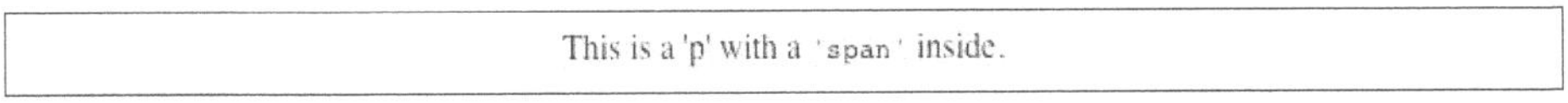

Figure 18. Monospace size oddities

The default value of medium is generally resolved to 16px, assuming the user hasn't changed the browser preferences (where the default text sizes are set). Indeed, if you query the paragraph text outside the span, inspectors will tell you that the computed font-size of the text is 16px (again, assuming the user hasn't changed the preferences).

So you might expect the monospaced span to also have 16 pixel text. That's exactly the case in some browsers, but in others, it will be 13px instead.

The reason for this is that while the computed font-size of the paragraph is 16px, the keyword medium is what's passed down through inheritance. Thus, the span starts out with font-size: medium. As a result, it looks to the user's preference settings to determine the proper size, and most browsers are set to a 13px default size for all mono-space text. This causes them to display 13-pixel monospace text in a 16-pixel parent, even though the monospace text was explicitly set to font-size: 1em.

The effect carries through even with font sizes other than 1em (or 100%); in the following case, the monospace text will have a computed size of 26px instead of 32px (once more assuming the browser defaults have not changed):

```
p {font-size: medium;}    /* the default value */
span {font-family: monospace; font-size: 2em;}

<p>This is a 'p' with a <span>'span'</span> inside.</p>
```

Note that not all browsers actually do this: some override the medium sizing assumptions in favor of scaling off the computed font-size of the parent. This leads to inconsistent text display across browsers.

As it happens, there is a way to work around this problem that works for all known browsers, at least as of early 2013. It goes like this:

```
p {font-size: medium;}    /* the default value */
span {font-family: monospace, serif; font-size: 1em;}

<p>This is a 'p' with a <span>'span'</span> inside.</p>
```

See the extra serif in the font-family there? That somehow triggers a switch that makes all browsers treat font-size: 1em as being 100% of the paragraph's computed font-size, not a medium-derived value. This is cross-browser-consistent and illustrated in Figure 19.

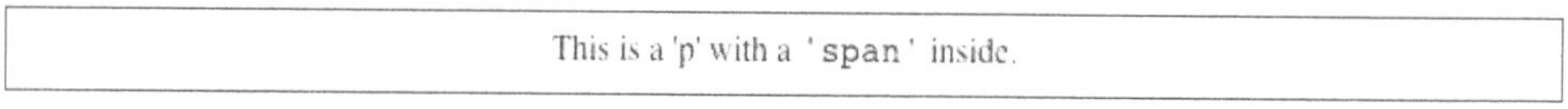

Figure 19. Monospace size harmony

Using Length Units

The font-size can be set using any length value. All of the following font-size dec-larations should be equivalent:

```
p.one {font-size: 36pt;}
p.two {font-size: 3pc;}
p.three {font-size: 0.5in;}
p.four {font-size: 1.27cm;}
p.five {font-size: 12.7mm;}
```

The display in Figure 20 assumes that the user agent knows how many dots per inch are used in the display medium. Different user agents make different assumptions—some based on the operating system, some based on preferences settings, and some based on the assumptions of the programmer who wrote the user agent. Nevertheless, the five lines should always have the same font size. Thus, while the result may not exactly match reality (for example, the actual size of `p.three` may not be half an inch), the measurements should all be consistent with one another.

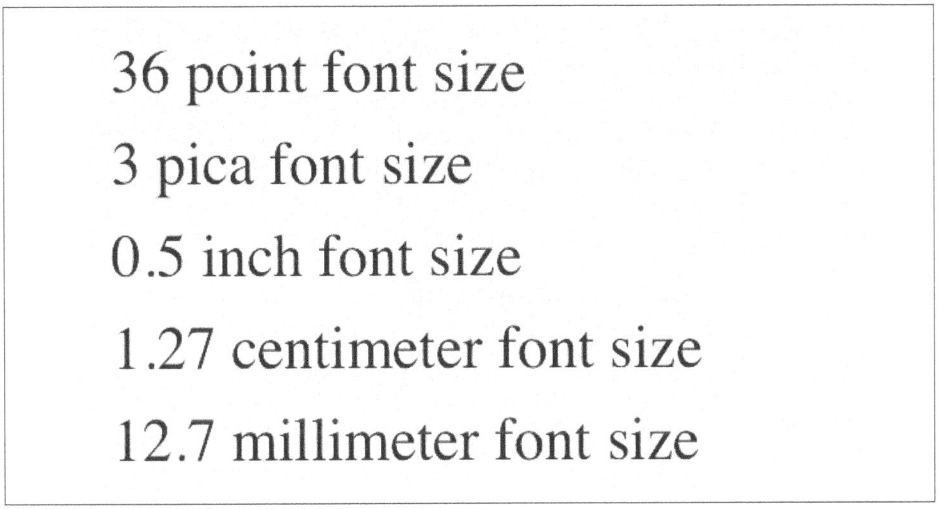

36 point font size

3 pica font size

0.5 inch font size

1.27 centimeter font size

12.7 millimeter font size

Figure 20. Various font sizes

There is one more value that is potentially the same as those shown in Figure 20, and that's `36px`, which would be the same physical distance if the display medium is 72 pixels-per-inch (ppi). However, there are very few monitors with that setting anymore. Most desktop displays are much higher, in the range of 96ppi to 120ppi; and mobile devices go much higher, currently in the 300ppi – 500ppi range.

Despite these variations between operating systems and devices, many authors choose to use pixel values for font sizes. This approach seems especially attractive when mixing text and raster images (GIF, JPG, PNG, etc.) on a web page, since text can (in theory) be set to the same height as graphic elements on the page by declaring `font-size: 11px;` or something similar, as illustrated by Figure 21.

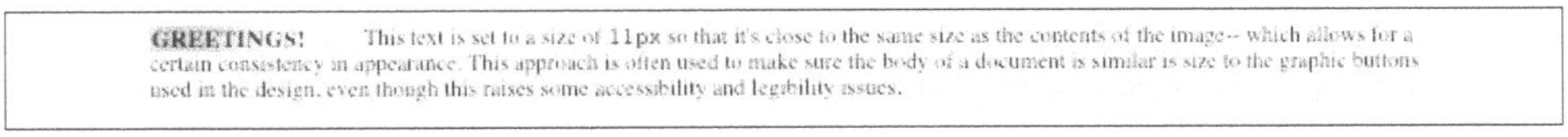

GREETINGS!   This text is set to a size of 11px so that it's close to the same size as the contents of the image— which allows for a certain consistency in appearance. This approach is often used to make sure the body of a document is similar is size to the graphic buttons used in the design, even though this raises some accessibility and legibility issues.

Figure 21. Keeping text and graphics in scale with pixel sizes

Using pixel measurements for `font-size` is certainly one way to get "consistent" results with `font-size` (and, indeed, with any length at all), but there is a drawback. Not every browser makes it easy (or even possible) to resize text set in pixels, and there are situations where pixel-sized text can be badly sized in mobile devices that pretend to be full-screen devices (such as most versions of the iPhone). For these reasons alone, pixel-sizing text is generally not recommended.

Automatically Adjusting Size

Two of the main factors that influence a font's legibility are its size and its x-height. The number that results from dividing the x-height by the `font-size` is referred to as the *aspect value*. Fonts with higher aspect values tend to be legible as the font's size is reduced; conversely, fonts with low aspect values become illegible more quickly. CSS provides a way to deal with shifts in aspect values between font families with the property `font-size-adjust`.

---

font-size-adjust

Values:
    `<number>` | none | auto | inherit

Initial value:
    none

Applies to:
    All elements

Inherited:
    Yes

The goal of this property is to preserve legibility when the font used is not the author's first choice. Because of the differences in font appearance, while one font may be legible at a certain size, another font at the same size is difficult or impossible to read.

A good example is to compare the common fonts Verdana and Times. Consider Figure 22 and the following markup, which shows both fonts at a `font-size` of `10px`:

```
p {font-size: 10px;}
p.cl1 {font-family: Verdana, sans-serif;}
p.cl2 {font-family: Times, serif; }
```

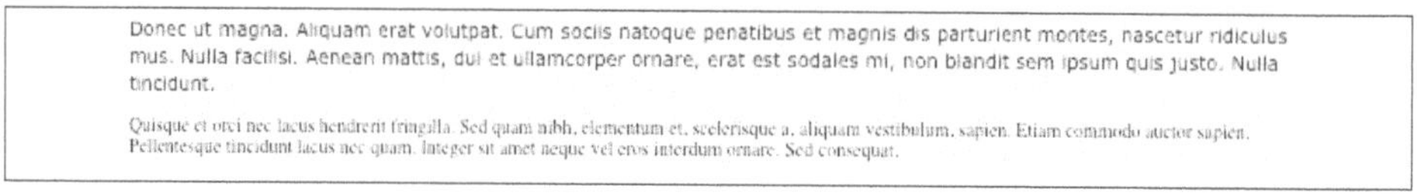

Donec ut magna. Aliquam erat volutpat. Cum sociis natoque penatibus et magnis dis parturient montes, nascetur ridiculus mus. Nulla facilisi. Aenean mattis, dui et ullamcorper ornare, erat est sodales mi, non blandit sem ipsum quis justo. Nulla tincidunt.

Quisque et orci nec lacus hendrerit fringilla. Sed quam nibh, elementum et, scelerisque a, aliquam vestibulum, sapien. Etiam commodo auctor sapien. Pellentesque tincidunt lacus nec quam. Integer sit amet neque vel eros interdum ornare. Sed consequat.

Figure 22. Comparing Verdana and Times

The text in Times is much harder to read than the Verdana text. This is partly due to the limitations of pixel-based display, but it is also because Times simply becomes harder to read at smaller font sizes.

As it turns out, the ratio of x-height to character size in Verdana is 0.58, whereas in Times it is 0.46. What you can do in this case is declare the aspect value of Verdana, and the user agent will adjust the size of the text that's actually used. This is accomplished using the formula:

Declared `font-size` × (`font-size-adjust` value ÷ aspect value of available font) = Adjusted `font-size`

So, in a situation where Times is used instead of Verdana, the adjustment is as follows:

```
10px × (0.58 ÷ 0.46) = 12.6px
```

which leads to the result shown in Figure 23:

```
p {font: 10px Verdana, sans-serif; font-size-adjust: 0.58;}
p.cl2 {font-family: Times, serif; }
```

Donec ut magna. Aliquam erat volutpat. Cum sociis natoque penatibus et magnis dis parturient montes, nascetur ridiculus mus. Nulla facilisi. Aenean mattis, dui et ullamcorper ornare, erat est sodales mi, non blandit sem ipsum quis justo. Nulla tincidunt.

Quisque et orci nec lacus hendrerit fringilla. Sed quam nibh, elementum et, scelerisque a, aliquam vestibulum, sapien. Etiam commodo auctor sapien. Pellentesque tincidunt lacus nec quam. Integer sit amet neque vel eros interdum ornare. Sed consequat.

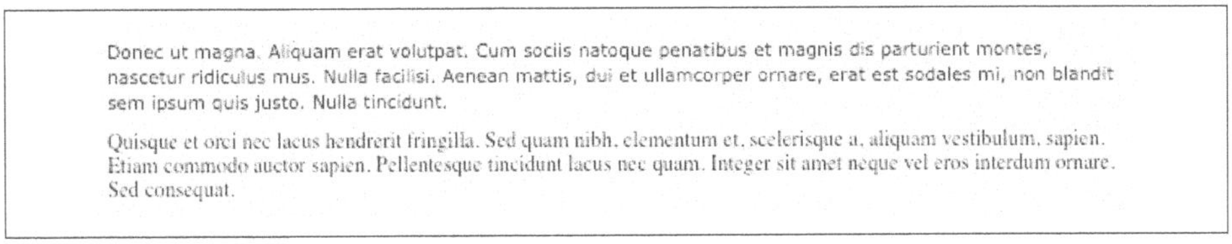

Figure 23. Adjusting Times

Of course, to allow a user agent to intelligently make size adjustments, it first has to know the aspect value of the fonts you specify. User agents that support `@font-face` will be able to pull that information directly from the font file, assuming the files contain the information—any professionally-produced font should, but there's no guarantee. If a font file doesn't contain the aspect value, a user agent may try to compute it, but again, there's no guarantee that they will or even can.

Assuming that the user agent can find or figure out aspect values, the `auto` value for `font-size-adjust` is a way of getting the desired effect even if you don't know the actual aspect value of your first-choice font. For example, given that the user agent can determine that the aspect value of Verdana is 0.58, then the following will have the same result as that shown in Figure 23:

```
p {font: 10px Verdana, sans-serif; font-size-adjust: auto;}
p.cl2 {font-family: Times, serif; }
```

Declaring `font-size-adjust: none;` will, obviously, suppress any adjustment of font sizes. This is the default state.

As of early 2013, the only user agent line to support `font-size-adjust` was the Gecko family.

Font Style

`font-style` is very simple: it's used to select between `normal` text, `italic` text, and `oblique` text. That's it! The only complication is in recognizing the difference between `italic` and `oblique` text and in understanding why browsers don't always give you a choice.

---

font-style

Values:
    `italic | oblique | normal | inherit`

Initial value:
    `normal`

Applies to:
    All elements

Inherited:
    Yes

Computed value:
    As specified

Note:
    Has a corresponding `@font-face` descriptor (see below)

The default value of `font-style` is, as you can see, `normal`. This refers to "upright" text, which is probably best described as "text that is not italic or otherwise slanted." The vast majority of text in this book is upright, for instance. That leaves only an explanation of the difference between `italic` and `oblique` text. For that, it's easiest to refer to Figure 24, which illustrates the differences very clearly.

Basically, italic text is a separate font face, with small changes made to the structure of each letter to account for the altered appearance. This is especially true of serif fonts, where, in addition to the fact that the text characters "lean," the serifs may be altered in an italic face. Oblique text, on the other hand, is simply a slanted version of the normal, upright text. Font faces with labels like "Italic," "Cursive," and "Kursiv" are usually mapped to the `italic` keyword, while `oblique` is often assigned faces with labels such as "Oblique," "Slanted," and "Incline."

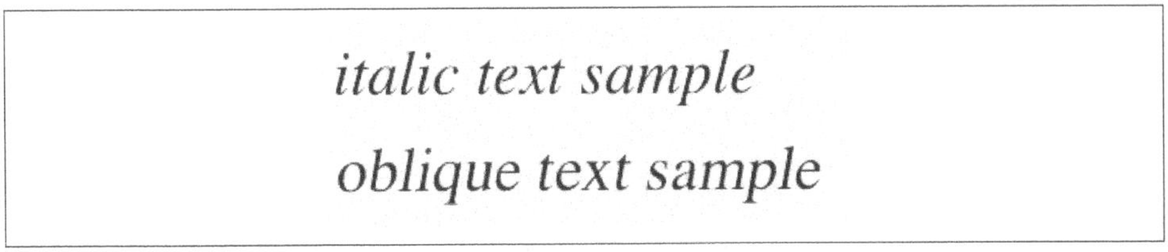

Figure 24. Italic and oblique text in detail

If you want to make sure that a document uses italic text in familiar ways, you could write a style sheet like this:

```
p {font-style: normal;}
em, i {font-style: italic;}
```

These styles would make paragraphs use an upright font, as usual, and cause the em and i elements to use an italic font—again, as usual. On the other hand, you might decide that there should be a subtle difference between em and i:

```
p {font-style: normal;}
em {font-style: oblique;}
i {font-style: italic;}
```

If you look closely at Figure 25, you'll see there is no apparent difference between the em and i elements. In practice, not every font is so sophisticated as to have both an italic face and an oblique face, and even fewer web browsers are sophisticated enough to tell the difference when both faces do exist.

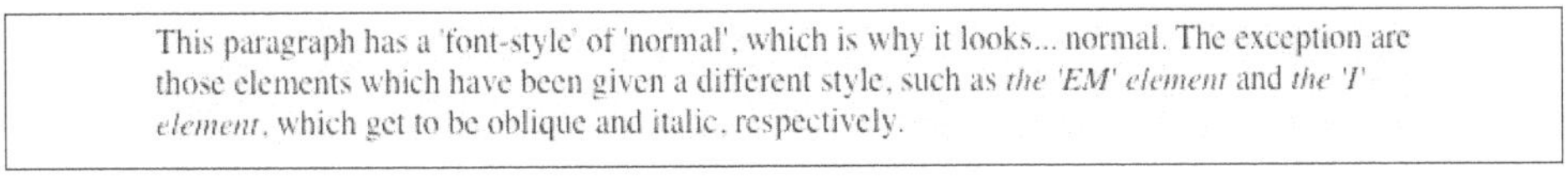

Figure 25. More font styles

If either of these is the case, then there are a few things that can happen. If there is no "Italic" face available, but there is an "Oblique" face, then the latter can be used for the former. If the situation is reversed—an "Italic" face exists, but there is no defined "Oblique" face—the user agent may *not* substitute the former for the latter, according to the specification. Finally, the user agent can simply generate the oblique face by computing a slanted version of the upright font. In fact, this is what most often happens in a digital world, where it's fairly simple to slant a font using a simple computation.

Furthermore, you may find that in some operating systems, a given font that has been declared as italic may switch from italic to oblique depending on the actual size of the font. The display of Times on a Macintosh running the Classic OS (Mac OS 9), for example, is shown in Figure 26, where the only difference is a single pixel in font size.

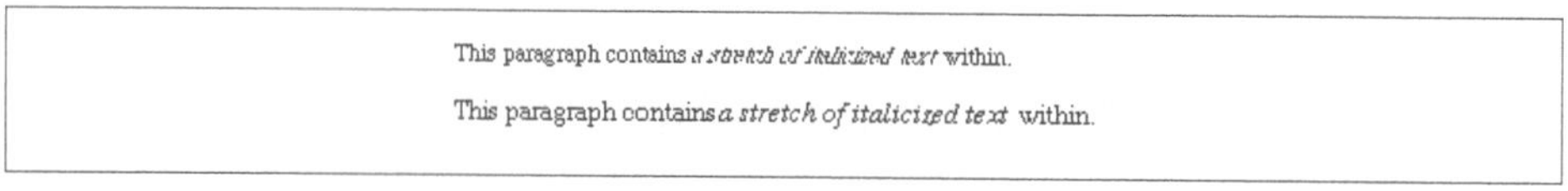

Figure 26. Same font, same style, different sizes

There isn't much that can be done about this, unfortunately, except better font handling. Fortunately, modern operating systems such as Mac OS X and Windows XP have very good font rendering technology, and @font-face allows authors to assign specific italic and oblique faces to the respective font-style properties, should they so choose.

Even though italic and oblique text often use the same face, font-style can still be quite useful. For example, it is a common typographic convention that a block quote should be italicized, but that any specially emphasized text within the quote should be upright. To employ this effect, which is illustrated in Figure 27, you would use these styles:

```
blockquote {font-style: italic;}
blockquote em, blockquote i {font-style: normal;}
```

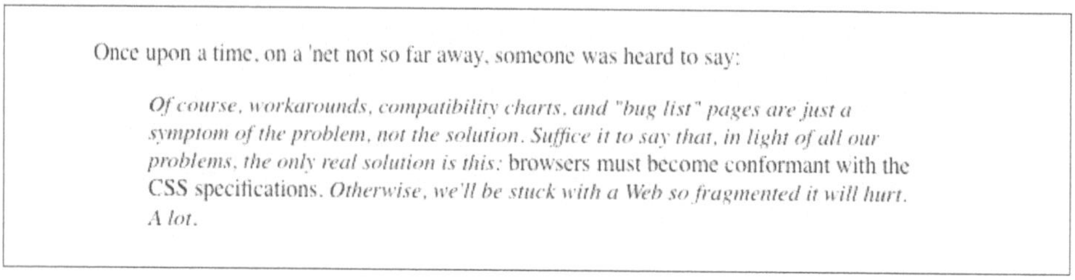

Figure 27. Common typographical conventions through CSS

A related property tells the user agent whether it's allowed to synthesize its own bold or italic faces when a family doesn't contain them.

The font-style Descriptor

As a descriptor, font-style lets an author link specific faces to specific font-style values.

```
@font-face {
    font-family: "SwitzeraADF";
    font-style: normal;
    src: url("SwitzeraADF-Regular.otf") format("opentype");
}
@font-face {
    font-family: "SwitzeraADF";
    font-style: italic;
    src: url("SwitzeraADF-Italic.otf") format("opentype");
}
```

```
@font-face {
    font-family: "SwitzeraADF";
    font-style: oblique;
    src: url("SwitzeraADF-Italic.otf") format("opentype");
}
```

Given the above, the result of the following rules would be to render h2 and h3 elements using "SwitzeraADF-Italic" instead of "SwitzeraADF-Regular," as illustrated in Figure 28:

```
h1, h2, h3 {font: 225% SwitzeraADF, Helvetica, sans-serif;}
h2 {font-size: 180%; font-style: italic;}
h3 {font-size: 150%; font-style: oblique;}
```

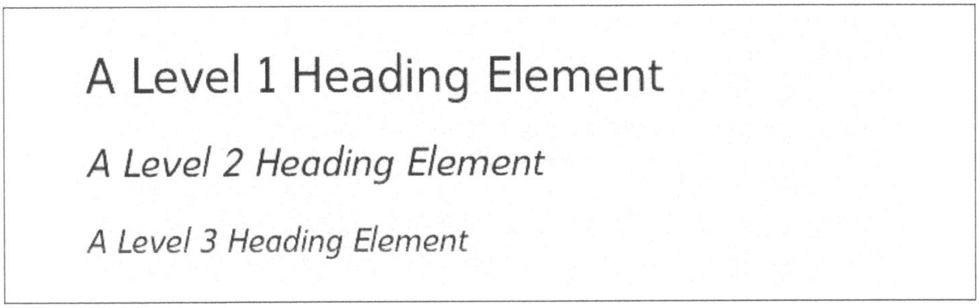

A Level 1 Heading Element

A Level 2 Heading Element

A Level 3 Heading Element

Figure 28. Using declared font-style faces

Of course, if there were a SwitzeraADF face with an oblique typeface, the author could point to it instead of the italic variant. There isn't such a face, though, so the author mapped the italic face to both the `italic` and `oblique` values. As with `font-weight`, the `font-style` descriptor can take all of the values of the `font-style` property *except* for `inherit`.

Font Stretching

In some font families, there are a number of variant faces that have wider or narrower letterforms. These often take names like "Condensed," "Wide," "Ultra Expanded," and so on. The utility of such variants is that a designer can use a single font family while also having skinny and fat variants. CSS provides a property that allows an author to select among such variants, when they exist, without having to explicitly define them in `font-family` declarations. It does this via the somewhat misleadingly named `font-stretch`.

font-stretch

Values:

normal | ultra-condensed | extra-condensed | condensed | semi-condensed |
semi-expanded | expanded | extra-expanded | ultra-expanded | inherit

Initial value:

normal

Applies to:

All elements

Inherited:

Yes

Note:

Has a corresponding @font-face descriptor (see below)

You might expect from the property name that this will stretch or squeeze a font like saltwater taffy, but that's actually not the case at all. As the value names imply, this property instead behaves very much like the absolute-size keywords (e.g., xx-large) for the font-size property, with a range of absolute values that (in theory) let the author alter a font's width. For example, an author might decide to stress the text in a strongly emphasized element by changing the font characters to a wider face than their parent element's font characters.

The catch is that this property only works if the font family in use has defined wider and narrower faces, which most do not (and those that do are usually very expensive). Thus this property is actually very different from font-size, which can change the size of any font face at any time. In contrast, declaring font-stretch: expanded will only have an effect if the font in use has an expanded face available. If it doesn't, then nothing will happen: the font's face will not change.

For example, consider the very common font Verdana, which has only one width face; this is equivalent to font-stretch: normal. Declaring the following will have no effect on the width of the displayed text:

```
body {font-family: Verdana;}
strong {font-stretch: extra-expanded;}
footer {font-stretch: extra-condensed;}
```

All of the text will be at Verdana's usual width. However, if the font family is changed to one that has a number of width faces, such as Futura, then things will be different, as shown in Figure 29:

```
body {font-family: Verdana;}
strong {font-stretch: extra-expanded;}
footer {font-stretch: extra-condensed;}
```

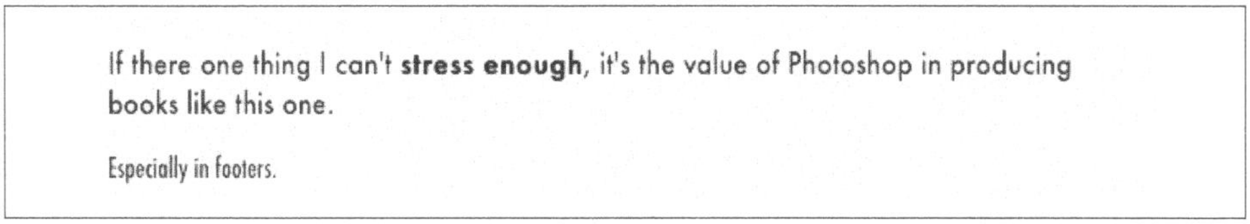

If there one thing I can't **stress enough**, it's the value of Photoshop in producing books like this one.

Especially in footers.

Figure 29. Stretching font characters

 As of early 2013, only Gecko-based browsers and Internet Explorer 9+ supported font-stretch. Furthermore, as noted, they only supported it for font families that have variant faces available.

The font-stretch Descriptor

Much as with the font-weight descriptor, the font-stretch descriptor allows authors to explicitly assign faces of varying widths to the width values permitted in the font-stretch property. For example, the following rules explicitly assign three faces to the most directly analogous font-stretch values:

```
@font-face {
    font-family: "SwitzeraADF";
    font-stretch: normal;
    src: url("SwitzeraADF-Regular.otf") format("opentype");
}
@font-face {
    font-family: "SwitzeraADF";
    font-stretch: condensed;
    src: url("SwitzeraADF-Cond.otf") format("opentype");
}
@font-face {
    font-family: "SwitzeraADF";
    font-stretch: expanded;
    src: url("SwitzeraADF-Ext.otf") format("opentype");
}
```

In a parallel to what we saw in previous sections, the author can call on these different width faces through the font-stretch property, as illustrated in Figure 30:

```
h1, h2, h3 {font: 225% SwitzeraADF, Helvetica, sans-serif;}
h2 {font-size: 180%; font-stretch: condensed;}
h3 {font-size: 150%; font-stretch: expanded;}
```

As before, the font-stretch descriptor can take all of the values of the font-stretch property *except* for inherit.

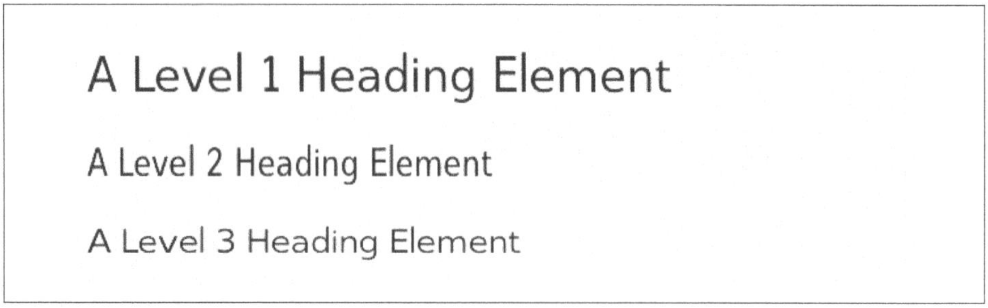

Figure 30. Using declared font-stretch faces

Font Kerning

Some fonts contain data regarding how characters should be spaced relative to each other, known as *kerning*. This spacing can vary depending on how characters are combined; for example, the character pair "oc" may have a different spacing than the pair "ox." Similarly, "AB" and "AW" may have different separation distances, to the point that in some fonts, the top-right tip of the "W" is actually placed to the left of the bottom-right tip of the "A." This kerning data can be explicitly called for or suppressed using the property `font-kerning`.

font-kerning

Values:
    auto | normal | none | inherit

Initial value:
    auto

Applies to:
    All elements

Inherited:
    Yes

The value `none` is pretty obvious: it tells the user agent to ignore any kerning information in the font. `normal` tells the user agent to kern the text normally; that is, according to the kerning data contained in the font. `auto` tells the user agent to do whatever it thinks best, possibly depending on the type of font in use. The OpenType specification, for example, recommends (but does not require) that kerning be applied whenever the font supports it. If a font does not contain kerning data, of course, `font-kerning` will have no effect.

Note that if the property letter-spacing is applied to kerned text, the kerning is done and *then* the letters' spacing is adjusted according to the value of letter-spacing, not the other way around.

Font Variants

Beyond font weights, font styles, and so forth, there are font variants. These are embedded within a font face and can cover things like various styles of historical ligatures, small-caps presentation, ways of presenting fractions, the spacing of numbers, whether zeroes get slashes through them, and much more. CSS lets authors invoke these variants, when they exist, through font-variant.

---

font-variant

Values (CSS2.1):
normal | small-caps

Values (Level 3):
normal | none | [*<common-lig-values>* || *<discretionary-lig-values>* || *<historical-lig-values>* || *<contextual-alt-values>* || stylistic(*<feature-value-name>*) || historical-forms || styleset(*<feature-value-name>*#) || character-variant(*<feature-value-name>*#) || swash(*<feature-value-name>*) || ornaments(*<feature-value-name>*) || annotation(*<feature-value-name>*) || [small-caps | all-small-caps | petite-caps | all-petite-caps | unicase | titling-caps] || *<numeric-figure-values>* || *<numeric-spacing-values>* || *<numeric-fraction-values>* || ordinal || slashed-zero || *<east-asian-variant-values>* || *<east-asian-width-values>* || ruby] | inherit

Initial value:
normal

Applies to:
All elements

Inherited:
Yes

Computed value:
As specified

Note:
Has a corresponding @font-face descriptor (see below)

That's quite a "Values (Level 3)" entry, isn't it? Especially when the only values in CSS1 and CSS2 were the default of normal, which describes ordinary text, and small-caps, which calls for the use of small-caps text. Let's concentrate just on those for a moment.

Instead of upper- and lowercase letters, a small-caps font employs uppercase letters of different sizes. Thus, you might see something like that shown in Figure 31:

```
h1 {font-variant: small-caps;}
h1 code, p {font-variant: normal;}

<h1>The Uses of <code>font-variant</code> On the Web</h1>
<p>
The property <code>font-variant</code> is very interesting...
</p>
```

THE USES OF font-variant

The property font-variant is very interesting. Given how common its use is in print media and the relative ease of its implementation, it should be supported by every CSS1-aware browser.

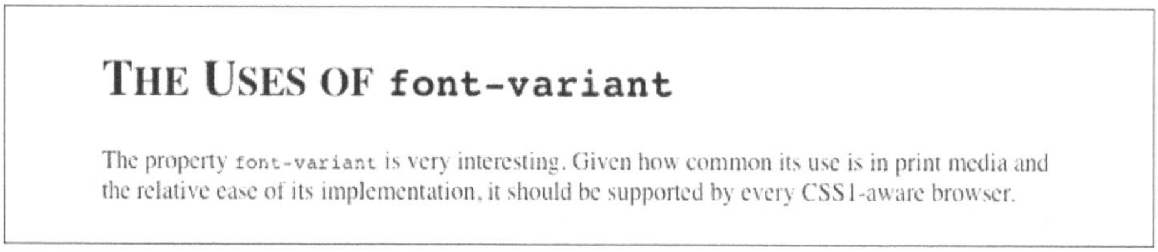

Figure 31. The small-caps value in use

As you may notice, in the display of the h1 element, there is a larger uppercase letter wherever an uppercase letter appears in the source and a small uppercase letter wherever there is a lowercase letter in the source. This is very similar to text-transform: upper case, with the only real difference being that, here, the uppercase letters are of different sizes. However, the reason that small-caps is declared using a font property is that some fonts have a specific small-caps face, which a font property is used to select.

What happens if no such face exists? There are two options provided in the specification. The first is for the user agent to create a small-caps face by scaling uppercase letters on its own. The second is simply to make all letters uppercase and the same size, exactly as if the declaration text-transform: uppercase; had been used instead. This is obviously not an ideal solution, but it is permitted.

 Internet Explorer for Windows took the all-caps route before IE6. Most other browsers display small-caps text when asked to do so.

Level 3 Values

Now to examine that "Values (Level 3)" line. It is admittedly complicated, but there's an easy way to explain it. It's actually a shorthand for all the values permitted for the following properties:

- `font-variant-ligatures`
- `font-variant-caps`
- `font-variant-numeric`
- `font-variant-alternates`
- `font-variant-east-asian`

As an example (to pick one of the simpler ones), `<common-lig-values>` comes from the property `font-variant-ligatures`, and can be either `common-ligatures` or `no-common-ligatures`. `<numeric-fraction-values>` comes from `font-variant-numeric` and can be either `diagonal-fractions` or `stacked-fractions`. And so on.

There are two barriers to the use of these admittedly much more powerful font variants: browser support and font support. The first is easy: as of mid-2013, there isn't widespread support for enabling font variants. Certainly you can use the CSS 2.1 variant values, but many of the Level 3 values are only supported by Gecko.

The second is also easy while also being complex: not every font supports every variant. For example, most Latin fonts won't support any of the East Asian variants; for another, not every font will include support for, say, some of the numeric and ligature variants. To find out what a given font supports, you have to consult its documentation, or do a lot of testing no documentation is available. (Most commercial fonts do come with documentation, and most free fonts don't.)

The main thing to keep in mind is that even if a variant works in a given browser for one font, it may not for another; and just because a font has a given variant, that doesn't mean that all browsers will let you invoke it. So it's complicated, and there aren't many detailed guides to help out.

 The various `font-variant-*` properties are not covered in detail here because as of early 2013, they were not well supported in browsers. For more details, see *http://w3.org/TR/css3-fonts/*.

The font-variant Descriptor

The `font-variant` descriptor lets you decide which of a font face's variants can or cannot be used, specified as a space-separated list. For example, you can enable the common ligature, small caps, and slashed-zeroes variants like so:

```
font-variant: common-ligatures small-caps slashed-zero;
```

You'll no doubt have guessed by now that the `font-variant` descriptor can take all of the values of the `font-variant` property *except* for `inherit`.

Note that this descriptor is very different than the other descriptors we've seen so far. With the `font-stretch` descriptor, for example, you can assign a specific font face to a given `font-stretch` property value. The `font-variant` descriptor, by contrast, defines which variants are permitted for the font face being declared in the `@font-face` rule, which can easily negate font variant values called for in properties later on. For example, given the following, paragraphs will *not* be displayed using a `diagonal-fractions` or `small-caps` variant, even if such variants exist in SwitzeraADF:

```
@font-face {
    font-family: "SwitzeraADF";
    font-weight: normal;
    src: url("SwitzeraADF-Regular.otf") format("opentype");
    font-variant: stacked-fractions titling-caps slashed-zero;
}

p {font: small-caps 1em SwitzeraADF, sans-serif; font-variant-numeric: diagonal-fractions;}
```

Font Features

In a manner similar to `font-variant`, the `font-feature-settings` descriptor allows authors to exercise low-level control over which OpenType font features are available for use (so don't go using this descriptor on `.woff` files).

---

font-feature-settings

Values:
    `normal` | *<feature-tag-value>*# | `inherit`

Initial value:
    `normal`

Note:
    Has a corresponding `@font-face` descriptor (see below)

You can list one or more comma-separated OpenType features, as defined by the Open-Type specification. For example, enabling common ligatures, small caps, and slashed zeroes would look something like this:

```
font-feature-settings: "liga" on, "smcp" on, "zero" on;
```

The exact format of a *<feature-tag-value>* value is:

<feature-tag-value>
    <string> [*<integer>* | on | off]?

For many features, the only permitted integer values are 0 and 1, which are equivalent to off and on (and vice versa). There are some features that allow a range of numbers, however, in which case values greater than 1 both enable the feature and define the feature's selection index. If a feature is listed but no number is provided, 1 (on) is assumed. Thus, the following descriptors are all equivalent:

```
font-feature-settings: "liga";      /* 1 is assumed */
font-feature-settings: "liga" 1;    /* 1 is declared */
font-feature-settings: "liga" on;   /* on = 1 */
```

Remember that all *<string>* values *must* be quoted. Thus, the first of the following descriptors will be recognized, but the second will be ignored:

```
font-feature-settings: "liga", dlig;
/* common ligatures are enabled; we wanted discretionary ligatures, but forgot
quotes */
```

A further restriction is that OpenType requires that all feature tags be four ASCII characters long. Any feature name longer or shorter, or that uses non-ASCII characters, is invalid and will be ignored. (This isn't something you personally need to worry about unless you're using a font that has it own made-up feature names and the font's creator didn't follow the naming rules.)

By default, OpenType fonts *always* have the following features enabled unless the author explicitly disables them via font-feature-settings or font-variant:

calt
    Contextual alternates

ccmp
    Composed characters

clig
    Contextual ligatures

liga
    Standard ligatures

locl
    Localized forms

mark
    Mark to base positioning

mkmk

Mark to mark positioning

rlig

Required ligatures

Additionally, other features may be enabled by default in specific situations, such as vert (Vertical alternates) for vertical runs of text.

 A complete list of standard OpenType feature names can be found at *http://microsoft.com/typography/otspec/featurelist.htm.*

The font-feature-settings Descriptor

The font-feature-settings descriptor lets you decide which of an OpenType font face's settings can or cannot be used, specified as a space-separated list.

Now, hold up a second—isn't that almost exactly what we did with font-variant just a few paragraphs ago? As a matter of fact, yes, it is. The font-variant descriptor covers nearly everything font-feature-settings does, plus a little more besides. It simply does so in a more CSS-like way, with value names instead of cryptic OpenType identifiers and Boolean toggles. Because of this, the CSS specification explicitly encourages authors to use font-variant instead of font-feature-settings, except in those cases where there's a font feature that the value list of font-variant doesn't include.

Keep in mind that this descriptor merely makes features available for use (or suppresses their use). It does not actually turn them on for the display of text; for that, see the section on the font-feature-settings property, described above.

Just as with the font-variant descriptor, the font-feature-settings descriptor defines which font features are permitted for the font face being declared in the @font-face rule. This can easily negate font feature values called for in properties later on. For example, given the following, paragraphs will *not* be displayed using alternative fractions nor small-caps, even if such features exist in SwitzeraADF:

```
@font-face {
    font-family: "SwitzeraADF";
    font-weight: normal;
    src: url("SwitzeraADF-Regular.otf") format("opentype");
    font-feature-settings: "afrc" off, "smcp" off;
}

p {font: 1em SwitzeraADF, sans-serif; font-feature-settings: "afrc", "smcp";}
```

As always, the font-feature-settings descriptor can take all of the values of the font-feature-settings property *except* for inherit.

Font Synthesis

It is sometimes the case that a given font family will lack alternate faces for things like bold or italic text. In such situations, the user agent may attempt to synthesize a face from the faces it has available, but this can lead to unattractive letterforms. To address this, CSS offers `font-synthesis`, which lets authors say how much synthesis they will or won't permit in the rendering of a page.

---

font-synthesis

Values:
    none | [weight || style] | inherit

Initial value:
    weight style

Applies to:
    All elements

Inherited:
    Yes

In many user agents, a font family that has no bold face can have one computed for it. This might be done by adding pixels to either side of each character glyph, for example. While this might seem useful, it can lead to results that are visually unappealing. This is why most font families actually have bold faces included: the font's designer wanted to make sure that bolded text in that font looked good.

Similarly, a font family that lacks an italic face an have one synthesized by simply slanting the characters in the normal face. This tends to look even worse than synthesized bold faces, particularly when it comes to serif fonts. Compare the difference between a synthesized italic version of Georgia (which we're calling "oblique" here) and the actual italic face included in Georgia, illustrated in Figure 32.

In supporting user agents, declaring `font-synthesis: none` blocks the user agent from doing any such synthesis for the affected elements. You can block it for the whole document with `html (font-synthesis: none;}`, for example. The downside is that any attempts to bold or italicize text using a font that doesn't offer the appropriate faces will stay unbolded or unitalicized. The upside is that you don't have to worry about a user agent trying to synthesize those variants and doing a poor job of it.

As of early 2013, there was no known user agent support for `font-synthesis`. It is included here mostly as a future-looking reference.

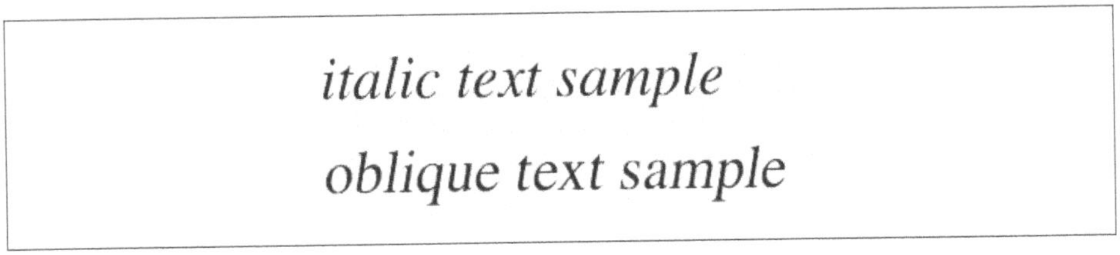

italic text sample

oblique text sample

Figure 32. Synthesized versus designed italics

The font Property

All of these properties are very sophisticated, of course, but using them all could get a little tedious:

```
h1 {font-family: Verdana, Helvetica, Arial, sans-serif; font-size: 30px;
    font-weight: 900; font-style: italic; font-variant: small-caps;}
h2 {font-family: Verdana, Helvetica, Arial, sans-serif; font-size: 24px;
    font-weight: bold; font-style: italic; font-variant: normal;}
```

Some of this problem could be solved by grouping selectors, but wouldn't it be easier to combine everything into a single property? Enter font, which is the shorthand property for all the other font properties (and a little more besides).

---

font

Values:
   [[*<font-style>* || [normal | small-caps] || *<font-weight>*]? *<font-size>*
   [/ *<line-height>*]? *<font-family>*] | caption | icon | menu | message-box |
   small-caption | status-bar | inherit

Initial value:
   Refer to individual properties

Applies to:
   All elements

Inherited:
   Yes

Percentages:
   Calculated with respect to the parent element for *<font-size>* and with respect to
   the element's *<font-size>* for *<line-height>*

Computed value:
   See individual properties (font-style, etc.)

Generally speaking, a font declaration can have any one value from each of the listed font properties, or else a "system font" value (described in "Using System Fonts" on page 55). Therefore, the preceding example could be shortened as follows (and have exactly the same effect, as illustrated by Figure 33):

```
h1 {font: italic 900 small-caps 30px Verdana, Helvetica, Arial, sans-serif;}
h2 {font: bold normal italic 24px Verdana, Helvetica, Arial, sans-serif;}
```

A LEVEL 1 HEADING ELEMENT

A Level 2 Heading Element

Figure 33. Typical font rules

I say that the styles "could be" shortened in this way because there are a few other possibilities, thanks to the relatively loose way in which font can be written. If you look closely at the preceding example, you'll see that the first three values don't occur in the same order. In the h1 rule, the first three values are the values for font-style, font-weight, and font-variant, in that order. In the second, they're ordered font-weight, font-variant, and font-style. There is nothing wrong here because these three can be written in any order. Furthermore, if any of them has a value of normal, that can be left out altogether. Therefore, the following rules are equivalent to the previous example:

```
h1 {font: italic 900 small-caps 30px Verdana, Helvetica, Arial, sans-serif;}
h2 {font: bold italic 24px Verdana, Helvetica, Arial, sans-serif;}
```

In this example, the value of normal was left out of the h2 rule, but the effect is exactly the same as in the preceding example.

It's important to realize, however, that this free-for-all situation applies only to the first three values of font. The last two are much stricter in their behavior. Not only must font-size and font-family appear in that order as the last two values in the declaration, but both must always be present in a font declaration. Period, end of story. If either is left out, then the entire rule will be invalidated and very likely to be ignored completely by a user agent. Thus, the following rules will get you the result shown in Figure 34:

```
h1 {font: normal normal italic 30px sans-serif;}   /*no problem here */
h2 {font: 1.5em sans-serif;}   /* also fine; omitted values set to 'normal' */
h3 {font: sans-serif;}   /* INVALID--no 'font-size' provided */
h4 {font: lighter 14px;}   /* INVALID--no 'font-family' provided */
```

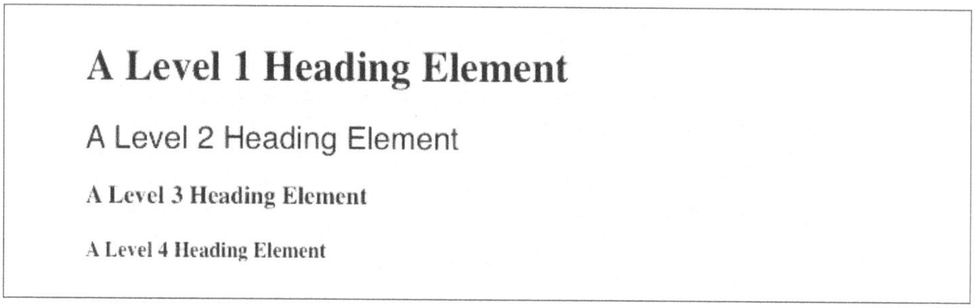

A Level 1 Heading Element

A Level 2 Heading Element

A Level 3 Heading Element

A Level 4 Heading Element

Figure 34. The necessity of both size and family

Adding the Line Height

So far, we've treated font as though it has only five values, which isn't quite true. It is also possible to set the value of the property line-height using font, despite that fact that line-height is a text property (not covered in this text), not a font property. It's done as a sort of addition to the font-size value, separated from it by a forward slash (/):

```
body {font-size: 12px;}
h2 {font: bold italic 200%/1.2 Verdana, Helvetica, Arial, sans-serif;}
```

These rules, demonstrated in Figure 35, set all h2 elements to be bold and italic (using face for one of the sans-serif font families), set the font-size to 24px (twice the body's size), and set the line-height to 28.8px.

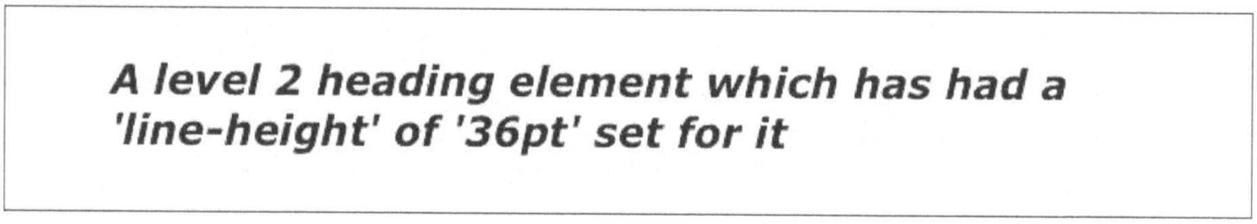

A level 2 heading element which has had a 'line-height' of '36pt' set for it

Figure 35. Adding line height to the mix

This addition of a value for line-height is entirely optional, just as the first three font values are. If you do include a line-height, remember that the font-size always comes before line-height, never after, and the two are always separated by a slash.

This may seem repetitive, but it's one of the most common errors made by CSS authors, so I can't say it enough: the required values for font are font-size and font-family, in that order. Everything else is strictly optional.

 line-height is discussed in detail in my upcoming book, *CSS Text Styling.*

Using Shorthands Properly

It is important to remember that font, being a shorthand property, can act in unexpected ways if you are careless with its use. Consider the following rules, which are illustrated in Figure 36:

```
h1, h2, h3 {font: italic small-caps 250% sans-serif;}
h2 {font: 200% sans-serif;}
h3 {font-size: 150%;}

<h1>This is an h1 element</h1>
<h2>This is an h2 element</h2>
<h3>This is an h3 element</h3>
```

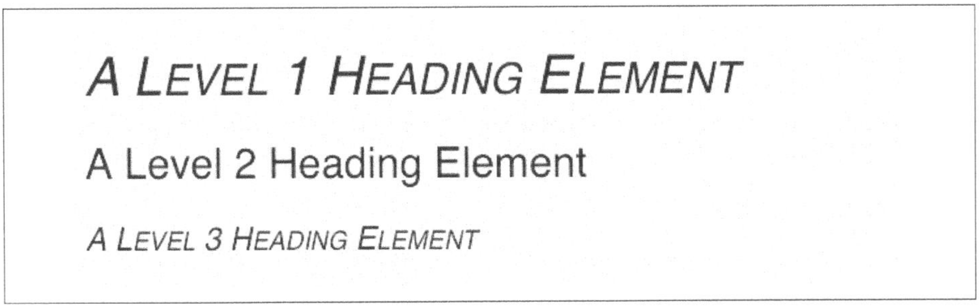

A LEVEL 1 HEADING ELEMENT

A Level 2 Heading Element

A LEVEL 3 HEADING ELEMENT

Figure 36. Shorthand changes

Did you notice that the h2 element is neither italicized nor small-capped, and that none of the elements are bold? This is the correct behavior. When the shorthand property font is used, any omitted values are reset to their defaults. Thus, the previous example could be written as follows and still be exactly equivalent:

```
h1, h2, h3 {font: italic normal small-caps 250% sans-serif;}
h2 {font: normal normal normal 200% sans-serif;}
h3 {font-size: 150%;}
```

This sets the h2 element's font style and variant to normal, and the font-weight of all three elements to normal. This is the expected behavior of shorthand properties. The h3 does not suffer the same fate as the h2 because you used the property font-size, which is not a shorthand property and therefore affects only its own value.

Using System Fonts

In situations where you want to make a web page "blend in" with the user's operating system, the system font values of font come in very handy. These are used to take the font size, family, weight, style, and variant of elements of the operating system, and apply them to an element. The values are as follows:

`caption`
> Used for captioned controls, such as buttons

`icon`
> Used to label icons

`menu`
> Used in menus—that is, drop-down menus and menu lists

`message-box`
> Used in dialog boxes

`small-caption`
> Used for labeling small controls

`status-bar`
> Used in window status bars

For example, you might want to set the font of a button to be the same as that of the buttons found in the operating system. For example:

```
button {font: caption;}
```

With these values, it is possible to create web-based applications that look very much like applications native to the user's operating system.

Note that system fonts may only be set as a whole; that is, the font family, size, weight, style, etc., are all set together. Therefore, the button text from our previous example will look exactly the same as button text in the operating system, whether or not the size matches any of the content around the button. You can, however, alter the individual values once the system font has been set. Thus, the following rule will make sure the button's font is the same size as its parent element's font:

```
button {font: caption; font-size: 1em;}
```

If you call for a system font and no such font exists on the user's machine, the user agent may try to find an approximation, such as reducing the size of the `caption` font to arrive at the `small-caption` font. If no such approximation is possible, then the user agent should use a default font of its own. If it can find a system font but can't read all of its values, then it should use the default value. For example, a user agent may be able to find a `status-bar` font but not get any information about whether the font is small-caps. In that case, the user agent will use the value `normal` for the `small-caps` property.

Font Matching

As we've seen, CSS allows for the matching of font families, weights, and variants. This is all accomplished through font matching, which is a vaguely complicated procedure. Understanding it is important for authors who want to help user agents make good font selections when displaying their documents. I left it for the end of the chapter because it's not really necessary to understand how the font properties work, and some readers will probably want to skip this part. If you're still interested, here's how font matching works:

1. The user agent creates, or otherwise accesses, a database of font properties. This database lists the various CSS properties of all of the fonts to which the user agent has access. Typically, this will be all fonts installed on the machine, although there could be others (for example, the user agent could have its own built-in fonts). If the user agent encounters two identical fonts, it will simply ignore one of them.

2. The user agent takes apart an element to which font properties have been applied and constructs a list of font properties necessary for the display of that element. Based on that list, the user agent makes an initial choice of a font family to use in displaying the element. If there is a complete match, then the user agent can use that font. Otherwise, it needs to do a little more work.

   a. A font is first matched against the `font-stretch` property.

   b. A font is next matched against the `font-style` property. The keyword `italic` is matched by any font that is labeled as either "italic" or "oblique." If neither is available, then the match fails.

   c. The next match is to `font-weight`, which can never fail thanks to the way `font-weight` is handled in CSS (explained earlier in the chapter).

   d. Then, `font-size` is tackled. This must be matched within a certain tolerance, but that tolerance is defined by the user agent. Thus, one user agent might allow matching within a 20 percent margin of error, whereas another might allow only 10 percent differences between the size specified and the size that is actually used.

3. If there was no font match in Step 2, the user agent looks for alternate fonts within the same font family. If it finds any, then it repeats Step 2 for that font.

4. Assuming a generic match has been found, but it doesn't contain everything needed to display a given element—the font is missing the copyright symbol, for instance—then the user agent goes back to Step 3, which entails a search for another alternate font and another trip through Step 2.

5. Finally, if no match has been made and all alternate fonts have been tried, then the user agent selects the default font for the given generic font family and does the best it can to display the element correctly.

Furthermore, the user agent does the following to resolve handling of font variants and features:

1. First, check for font features enabled by default, including features required for a given script. The core set of default-enabled features is: `"calt"`, `"ccmp"`, `"clig"`, `"liga"`, `"locl"`, `"mark"`, `"mkmk"`, `"rlig"`.

2. Then, if the font is defined via an `@font-face` rule, check for the features implied by the `font-variant` descriptor in the `@font-face` rule. Then check for the font features implied by the `font-feature-settings` descriptor in the `@font-face` rule.

3. Then check feature settings determined by properties other than `font-variant` or `font-feature-settings`. (For example, setting a non-default value for the `letter-spacing` property will disable ligatures.)

4. Then check for features implied by the value of the `font-variant` property, the related `font-variant` subproperties (e.g., `font-variant-ligatures`), and any other property that may call for the use of OpenType features (e.g., `font-kerning`).

5. Finally, check for the features implied by the value of `font-feature-settings` property.

The whole process is long and tedious, but it helps to understand how user agents pick the fonts they do. For example, you might specify the use of Times or any other serif font in a document:

```
body {font-family: Times, serif;}
```

For each element, the user agent should examine the characters in that element and determine whether Times can provide characters to match. In most cases, it can do so with no problem. Assume, however, that a Chinese character has been placed in the middle of a paragraph. Times has nothing that can match this character, so the user agent has to work around the character or look for another font that can fulfill the needs of displaying that element. Of course, any Western font is highly unlikely to contain Chinese characters, but should one exist (let's call it AsiaTimes), the user agent could use it in the display of that one element—or simply for the single character. Thus, the whole paragraph might be displayed using AsiaTimes, or everything in the paragraph might be in Times except for the single Chinese character, which is displayed in AsiaTimes.

Summary

From what was initially a very simplistic set of font properties, CSS has rapidly grown to allow fine-grained and wide-ranging influence over how fonts are displayed on the web. From custom fonts downloaded over the web to custom-built families assembled out of a variety of individual faces, authors may be fairly said to overflow with font power.

The typographic options available to authors today are far stronger than ever, but always remember: you must use this power wisely. While you can have seventeen different fonts in use on your site, that definitely doesn't mean that you should. Quite aside from the aesthetic difficulties this could present for your users, it would also make the total page weight much, much higher than it needs to be. As with any other aspect of web design, authors are advised to use their power wisely, not wildly.

About the Author

Eric A. Meyer has been working with the Web since late 1993 and is an internationally recognized expert on the subjects of HTML, CSS, and web standards. A widely read author, he is a past member of the CSS&FP Working Group and was the primary creator of the W3C's CSS1 Test Suite. In 2006, Eric was inducted into the International Academy of Digital Arts and Sciences for "international recognition on the topics of HTML and CSS" and helping to "inform excellence and efficiency on the Web."

Eric is currently the principal founder at Complex Spiral Consulting, which counts among its clients a wide variety of corporations, educational institutions, and government agencies. He is also, along with Jeffrey Zeldman, co-founder of An Event Apart ("The design conference for people who make websites"), and he speaks regularly at that conference as well as many others. Eric lives with his family in Cleveland, Ohio, which is a much nicer city than you've been led to believe. A historian by training and inclination, he enjoys a good meal whenever he can and considers almost every form of music to be worthwhile.

Colophon

The animal on the cover of *CSS Fonts* is a salmon (*Salmonidae* family).

The cover image is from the Dover Pictorial Archive. The cover font is Adobe ITC Garamond. The text font is Adobe Minion Pro; the heading font is Adobe Myriad Condensed; and the code font is Dalton Maag's Ubuntu Mono.

Get even more for your money.

Join the O'Reilly Community, and register the O'Reilly books you own. It's free, and you'll get:

- $4.99 ebook upgrade offer
- 40% upgrade offer on O'Reilly print books
- Membership discounts on books and events
- Free lifetime updates to ebooks and videos
- Multiple ebook formats, DRM FREE
- Participation in the O'Reilly community
- Newsletters
- Account management
- 100% Satisfaction Guarantee

Signing up is easy:

1. Go to: oreilly.com/go/register
2. Create an O'Reilly login.
3. Provide your address.
4. Register your books.

Note: English-language books only

To order books online:
oreilly.com/store

For questions about products or an order:
orders@oreilly.com

To sign up to get topic-specific email announcements and/or news about upcoming books, conferences, special offers, and new technologies:
elists@oreilly.com

For technical questions about book content:
booktech@oreilly.com

To submit new book proposals to our editors:
proposals@oreilly.com

O'Reilly books are available in multiple DRM-free ebook formats. For more information:
oreilly.com/ebooks

Spreading the knowledge of innovators   oreilly.com

Ingram Content Group UK Ltd.
Milton Keynes UK
UKHW032253240423
420706UK00009B/144

9 781449 371494